KT-133-098

Speakeasy Phrasemaker

ITALIAN

high
pines
press

CONTENTS

INDICE GENERALE

First Published in 1986

Published by
High Pines Press
PO Box 42
REIGATE
Surrey
RH2 8YW

ISBN 0 948792 04 3

Series devised and designed by
Peter Phillips

Cover drawing, maps and symbols by
Peter Phillips

Gesture Drawings by
Alison Archibald

Phototypeset by Southern Positives and Negatives (SPAN),
Lingfield, Surrey

Printed by Hazell Watson and Viney Ltd.,
Tring Road, Aylesbury, Bucks HP20 1LB

Other PHRASEMAKERS in this series
French
German
Spanish

In preparation
Danish
Dutch
Greek
Portuguese

INTRODUCTION

The SPEAKEASY PHRASEMAKER is a unique foreign-language translator, simpler to use than conventional phrasebooks and whose aim is quick and easy communication rather than unattainable lingustic perfection.

By building-up simple phrases from a collection of key words for particular subjects, it offers an almost infinate number of tailor-made phrases, and gives foreigners the opportunity to communicate back in a similar manner by pointing. The concept accepts that often inaccurate grammar is the price that has to be paid for this flexibility. The pronunciation, being especially designed for English speakers and having few rules, requires little prior study. Accuracy is again eshewed in preference for simplicity, yet it still enables adequate pronunciation to be achieved.

In addition to the usual phrasebook subjects, FAMILY RELATIONS, JOBS, SPORTS, HOBBIES, THE COUNTRYSIDE and HITCH-HIKING are also covered, which are handy for small talk or expanding the scope of other sections.

LAYOUT OF THE PHRASEMAKER

You'll find it easier to use the PHRASEMAKER if you familiarise yourself beforehand with how the various groups of subjects are sub-divided and where they are located throughout the book.

For quick reference, useful words and phrases are on the inside of the front cover. Even if Italians you meet understand English, most will appreciate your attempting a few words of greeting in their own language.

Most subjects are spread over double-pages. More complex ones, like EATING OUT, have additional pages following them, generally with lists of nouns, but you should always start any conversation at the 'starter' double-page.

The 'starter' pages of all subjects are laid out in a consistent pattern for familiarity. The left-hand page has a column of pronouns and negatives such as 'I you no' etc. down the left side; one or two columns of verbs in a 'box' at the top right-hand corner; a row of prepositions such as 'and at to' etc. along the bottom, and a few other useful words and phrases. The right-hand page has lists of adverbs, adjectives, relevant nouns and common signs related to the subject logically grouped together. A few sections eg. WEATHER, have all the above condensd onto a single page.

For quick reference, ACCIDENT, NUMBERS & ALPHABET and TIME & MEETING are located at the back, the latter including a unique clock enabling you to say time easily. GESTURE LANGUAGE is on page 59B. Across the bottom of most subject pages, there are useful cross-references to related subjects.

PHRASEMAKING

Make up phrases by pointing to words that have the nearest meaning to what you want to say. You can speak the translations as you point, using the phonetic pronunciation written in italics above the Italian. If you prefer not to speak, show the PHRASEMAKER to the person to whom you are talking and just point to the words. If you prefer to say the English whilst you are pointing that's fine too. Use whatever technique you find suits you best. Even if you attempt to speak the Italian, it would still help to let foreigners see what you are doing so that they will catch onto the idea and thus more able to answer back using the same technique. (The Italian text is in capitals to make it stand out against the pronunciation, so that the people you are conversing with can see the words they want to use clearly). There are a few simple instructions similar to these in Italian on the back cover which you can show people before inviting a reply.

Don't worry about the grammar, it will often sound like pigeon-English and will invariably sound pigeon-Italian to the listener, but providing you keep phrases short, use appropriate intonations and sometimes a little bit of sign language as well, you should be understood. When making questions, point to the question mark at the top left-hand corner of the subject 'starter' page first, and use an appropriate intonation when speaking.

English words that have different American and British meanings are followed by (UK) or (US) to distinguish them. Where a choice of English words is given, the second is always the American.

Here are examples of phrases using HOTEL-CHECKING IN AND OUT on page-10:

?   is there   cheap   Guest house   near   here
?   do you have   double room   for   (2)   night
?   HOW MUCH IS   bed & breakfast   per   night
?   do you have   more   good   room   with   private   bathroom

VERBS

The verb 'box' of most subjects begins with a group of 'would like's or 'want's followed by a group of 'have's' Where there are two of each, the first goes with 'I' and the second with 'you'. Where there are three of each, the middle one goes with 'we'. In other words they follow the same order as 'I we and you' in the first column. Note that 'would like' groups always finish with a 'want'. This goes with 'you' so one cannot say 'you would like'.

Where other personal pronouns such as 'he' and 'she' are included on a few of the pages, it is best to avoid using them with 'want' or 'have' if you can, as no special agreements have been provided for them with these verbs.

Except for 'is' and 'are' no other verbs require a choice. If you want to use an infinitive, eg. 'I want to pay', don't use 'to' even if it is listed in the prepositions, just say 'I want Pay'. Remember, keep it simple!

PRONUNCIATION

Read the pronunciation as if it were English but stress the syllables in bold type. If you can put a little Italian intonation into it – all the better! Don't be afraid to have a go!

Americans and Scots (who tend to roll their 'r's) should try not to sound single 'r's that follow an 'a', for example as in *settee-**mar**-na* (week). The 'r' is there is just to distinguish the 'a' as being like the 'a' in 'father' rather than as in 'cat'.

UPDATING

Much careful consideration has gone into the choice of words, range of subjects and reference data, and their disposition throughout the book for ease of use, but we would welcome any constructive comments and suggestions that you consider might help us to improve future editions.

Bon Voyage!

?

I	*ee-yo*	**IO**
we	*noy*	**NOI**
you	*lay-ee*	**LEI**

not	*non*	**NON**
no	*non*	**NON**

which	*kwar-lay*	**QUALE**
where	*doh-vay*	**DOVE**
what	*koh-sa*	**COSA**

how far	*kwan-toh dees-tan-tay*	**QUANTO DISTANTE**
how long	*kwan-toh tem-po*	**QUANTO TEMPO**
how many	*kwan-tee*	**QUANTI**

direction	*dee-retsee-yo-nay*	**DIREZIONE**

near	*vee-chee-no*	**VICINO**
here	*kwee*	**QUI**
there	*lar*	**LÀ**
this	*kwess-toh*	**QUESTO**
that	*kwel-lo*	**QUELLO**

want	*vol-yo*	**VOGLIO**
want	*vol-yar-mo*	**VOGLIAMO**
want	*vwar-lay*	**VUOLE**

is	*eh*	**È**
are	*so-no*	**SONO**
is there	*chay*	**C'È**

can I	*poss-o*	**POSSO**
can we	*possee-yar-mo*	**POSSIAMO**
can you	*pwoh*	**PUÒ**

Go	*an-dar-ray*	**ANDARE**
Show me	*mee-moss-tree*	**MI MOSTRI**
Tell me	*mee-dee-ka*	**MI DICA**
will Take	*pren-day*	**PRENDE**
Turn	*jee-rah-ray*	**GIRARE**
Write	*scree-vairray*	**SCRIVERE**

WRONG WAY! *strar-da sbal-yar-ta* **STRADA SBAGLIATA**

at	for	from	on	then	to
al	*pair*	*dah*	*soo*	*poyee*	*ah*
AL	**PER**	**DA**	**SU**	**POI**	**A**

tourist places etc: 18A   **road signs: 9A**

this place	*kwess-toh lwor-go* **QUESTO LUOGO**	nearest	*pee-yoo vee-chee-no* **PIÙ VICINO**
on map	*soo-la car-ta* **SULLA CARTA**	place	*no-may* **NOME**
		address	*eendee-reet-so* **INDIRIZZO**
next	*pross-eemo* **PROSSIMO**		
1st	*pree-mo* **1°**	about	*cheer-ka* **CIRCA**
2nd	*sek-on-doh* **2°**		
3rd	*tairt-so* **3°**	meters	*met-ree* **METRI**
4th	*kwar-toh* **4°**	kilometers	*kee-lo-metro* **CHILOMETRO**
5th	*kween-toh* **5°**		
turning	*vol-tar-ray* **VOLTARE**		
		minutes	*mee-noo-tee* **MINUTI**
at	*al* **AL**	hours	*or-ray* **ORE**
near	*vee-chee-no* **VICINO**		
before	*da-van-tee* **DAVANTI**	City centre	*chayn-tro chee-tah* **CENTRO CITTÀ**
after	*dor-po* **DOPO**	Junction	*een-kraw-cho* **INCROCIO**
then	*poyee* **POI**	Level/Railroad crossing	*pas-sar-jo ah lee-vel-lo* **PASSAGGIO A LIVELLO**
		Main road	*strar-da preenchee-par-lay* **STRADA PRINCIPALE**
left	*see-neess-tra* **SINISTRA**	Motorway/Freeway	*owtoh-strar-da* **AUTOSTRADA**
right	*dess-tra* **DESTRA**	Road	*strar-da* **STRADA**
slight angle	*pee-koh-la koor-vah* **PICCOLA CURVA**	Sign	*eendee-katsee-yo-nay* **INDICAZIONE**
straight ahead	*sem-pray dee-ree-toh* **SEMPRE DIRITTO**	Square	*pee-yat-sa* **PIAZZA**
again	*an-kor-rah* **ANCORA**	Street	*strar-da* **STRADA**
		Traffic lights	*semma-for-o* **SEMAFORO**
across	*attra-vair-so* **ATTRAVERSO**		
along	*loong-goh* **LUNGO**		
opposite	*dee fron-tay ah* **DI FRONTE A**	Toilets	*toy-let-tay* **TOILETTE**

?

I	*ee-yo*	**IO**
my	*eel **mee**-yo*	**IL MIO**
we	*noy*	**NOI**
you	*lay-ee*	**LEI**
not	*non*	**NON**
no	*non*	**NON**
which	*kwar-lay*	**QUALE**
where	*doh-vay*	**DOVE**
when	*kwan-doh*	**QUANDO**
what	*koh-sa*	**COSA**
what time	*kay or-ra*	**CHE ORA**
how long	*kwan-toh **tem**-po*	**QUANTO TEMPO**
how many	*kwan-tee*	**QUANTI**
near	*vee-**chee**-no*	**VICINO**
here	*kwee*	**QUI**
there	*lar*	**LÀ**
this	*kwess-toh*	**QUESTO**
these	*kwess-tee*	**QUESTI**

want	*vol-yo* **VOGLIO**		can I	*poss-o* **POSSO**	
want	*vol-**yar**-mo* **VOGLIAMO**		can I have	*poss-o ah-**vair**-ray* **POSSO AVERE**	
want	*vwar-lay* **VUOLE**		can we	*possee-**yar**-mo* **POSSIAMO**	
			can we have	*possee-**yar**-mo ah-**vair**-ray* **POSSIAMO AVERE**	
have	*oh* **HO**				
have	*abbee-**yar**-mo* **ABBIAMO**		Arrive	*arree-**var**-ray* **ARRIVARE**	
have	*ah* **HA**		Change	*kambee-**yar**-ray* **CAMBIARE**	
			Depart	*par-**teer**-ray* **PARTIRE**	
is	*eh* **È**		Go	*an-**dar**-ray* **ANDARE**	
are	*so-no* **SONO**		Rent	*affee-**tar**-ray* **AFFITTARE**	
is there	*chay* **C'È**		Wait	*aspair-**tar**-ray* **ASPETTARE**	

ticket	*beel-**yet**-toh* **BIGLIETTO**		1st class	*pree-ma **class**-ay* **PRIMA CLASSE**	
flight	*vol-lo* **VOLO**		business	*af-**far**-ree* **AFFARI**	
non-stop	*dee-**ret**-toh* **DIRETTO**		economy	*eckonom-**mee**-ya* **ECONOMIA**	
single	*an-**dar**-ta* **ANDATA**		front	*fron-tay* **FRONTE**	
return	*an-**dar**-ta eh ree-**tor**-no* **ANDATA E RITORNO**		back	*ah **ret**-roh* **A RETRO**	
person	*pair-**so**-na* **PERSONA**		middle	*met-so* **MEZZO**	
child/age	*bam-**bee**-no/et-**ta*** **BAMBINO ETÀ**		smoking	*foo-**mar**-ray* **FUMARE**	
seat	*poss-toh* **POSTO**		window	*fee-**ness**-tra* **FINESTRA**	

HOW MUCH IS (THAT)? *kwan-toh coss-ta* **QUANTO COSTA?**

at	by	for	form	in	on	to
al	*een*	*pair*	*dah*	*een*	*soo*	*ah*
AL	**IN**	**PER**	**DA**	**IN**	**SU**	**A**

directions: 1   **places & countries: 24 & 25**   **money & tipping: 50A**

journey	*vee-**yar**-jo* **VIAGGIO**	Flight No.	*noo-mairo dee **vol**-lo* **NUMERO DI VOLO**
first	*pree-mo* **PRIMO**	Aircraft	***air**-rayo* **AEREO**
last	*ool-teemo* **ULTIMO**	Check-in	*atchay-tatsee-yo-nay* **ACCETTAZIONE**
next	***pross**-eemo* **PROSSIMO**	Connection	*co-eenchee-**dent**-sa* **COINCIDENZA**
		Gate No.	*oo-**shee**-ta* **USCITA**
early	***press**-toh* **PRESTO**	Luggage	*bag-**gar**-lyee* **BAGAGLI**
late	*een ree-**tar**-doh* **IN RITARDO**	Take-off	*dek-**koh**-lo* **DECOLLO**
on time	*poontoo-**ar**-lay* **PUNTUALE**		
cancelled	*kanchel-**lar**-ray* **CANCELLARE**	Nothing to declare	***noo**-la da deekar-**rar**-ray* **NULLA DA DICHIARARE**
		Passport	*passa-**por**-toh* **PASSAPORTO**
minutes	*mee-**noo**-tee* **MINUTI**	Visa	***veess**-toh* **VISTO**
hours	***or**-ray* **ORE**		
days	***jor**-nee* **GIORNI**	Bank	***bang**-ka* **BANCA**
		Hotel reservation desk	*preno-tatsee-**yo**-nay al-**bair**-go* **PRENOTAZIONE ALBERGO**
open	*a-**pair**-toh* **APERTO**	Office	*oo-**fee**-cho* **UFFICIO**
closed	*kee-**oo**-zo* **CHIUSO**	Toilets	*toy-**let**-tay* **TOILETTE**
name	***no**-may* **NOME**	Airport bus	***owtoh**-boos delairo-**por**-toh* **AUTOBUS DELL'AEROPORTO**
address	*eendee-**reet**-so* **INDIRIZZO**	Car	*mak-**keena*** **MACCHINA**
		City centre	***chayn**-tro chee-**tah*** **CENTRO CITTÀ**
		Taxi	*taxi* **TAXI**

ARRIVO = ARRIVAL
PARTENZA = DEPARTURE
VIETATO FUMARE = NO SMOKING

Train	*tray-no* **TRENO**

?

I	*ee-yo* **IO**		
we	*noy* **NÓI**		
you	*lay-ee* **LÈI**		

want	*vol-yo* **VOGLIO**	can we	*possee-yar-mo* **POSSIAMO**
want	*vol-yar-mo* **VOGLIAMO**	can we have	*possee-yar-mo ah-vair-ay* **POSSIAMO AVERE**
want	*vwar-lay* **VUOLE**	can you	*pwoh* **PUÒ**

have	*oh* **HO**
have	*abbee-yar-mo* **ABBIAMO**
have	*ah* **HA**
is	*eh* **È**
are	*so-no* **SONO**
is there	*chay* **C'È**
can I	*poss-o* **POSSO**
can I have	*poss-o ah-vair-ay* **POSSO AVERE**

not	*non* **NON**
no	*non* **NON**
which	*kwar-lay* **QUALE**
where	*doh-vay* **DOVE**
what time	*kay or-ra* **CHE ORA**

Arrive	*arree-var-ray* **ARRIVARE**
Change	*cambee-yar-ray* **CAMBIARE**
Depart	*par-teer-ray* **PARTIRE**
Get off	*shen-dairay* **SCENDERE**
Go	*an-dar-ray* **ANDARE**
Show me	*mee moss-tree* **MI MOSTRI**
Tell me	*mee dee-ka* **MI DICA**
Wait	*aspair-tar-ray* **ASPETTARE**

how long	*kwan-toh tem-po* **QUANTO TEMPO**
how many	*kwan-tee* **QUANTI**
how often	*kwan-tay vol-tay* **QUANTE VOLTE**

single	*an-dar-ta* **ANDATA**
return	*an-dar-ta eh ree-tor-no* **ANDATA E RITORNO**
person	*pair-so-na* **PERSONA**
child	*bam-bee-no* **BAMBINO**
age	*et-ta* **ETÀ**

ticket	*beel-yet-toh* **BIGLIETTO**
book of tickets	*block-o dee beel-yet-ee* **BLOCCO DI BIGLIETTI**
reservation	*preno-tatsee-yo-nay* **PRENOTAZIONE**
small change	*speet-cho-lee* **SPICCIOLI**

near	*vee-chee-no* **VICINO**
here	*kwee* **QUI**
there	*lar* **LÀ**
this	*kwess-toh* **QUESTO**
these	*kwess-tee* **QUESTI**

STOP (HERE) *fair-mee (kwee)* **FERMI (QUI)**

HOW MUCH IS (THAT)? *kwan-toh coss-ta* **QUANTO COSTA?**

at	by	for	from	in	on	to
al **AL**	*een* **IN**	*pair* **PER**	*dah* **DA**	*een* **IN**	*soo* **SU**	*ah* **A**

tourist places: 18A   long-distance trains & buses: 4   time: 60

this place	*kwess-toh lwor-go* **QUESTO LUOGO**
nearest	*pee-yoo vee-chee-no* **PIÙ VICINO**
on map	*soo-la car-ta* **SULLA CARTA**
left	*see-neess-tra* **SINISTRA**
right	*dess-tra* **DESTRA**
straight ahead	*sem-pray dee-ree-toh* **SEMPRE DIRITTO**
first	*pree-mo* **PRIMO**
last	*ool-teemo* **ULTIMO**
next	*pross-eemo* **PROSSIMO**
early	*press-toh* **PRESTO**
late	*een ree-tar-doh* **IN RITARDO**
every	*on-yee* **OGNI**
per	*al* **AL**
minutes	*mee-noo-tee* **MINUTI**
hours	*or-ray* **ORE**
day	*jor-no* **GIORNO**
name	*no-may* **NOME**
address	*eendee-reet-so* **INDIRIZZO**

No.	*noo-mairo* **NUMERO**
Bus	*owtoh-boos* **AUTOBUS**
Metro	*metropolee-tar-na* **METROPOLITANA**
River bus	*moto-scar-fo* **MOTOSCAFO**
Taxi	*taxi* **TAXI**
Train	*tray-no* **TRENO**
Tram	*trarm* **TRAM**
Trolley bus	*fee-lo-boos* **FILOBUS**
Bus station	*statsee-yo-nay dowtoh-boos* **STAZIONE D'AUTOBUS**
Bus stop	*fair-mar-ta dowtoh-boos* **FERMATA D'AUTOBUS**
Jetty	*moh-lo* **MOLO**
Lost property	*oo-fee-cho od-jet-tee smar-eetee* **UFFICIO OGGETTI SMARRITI**
Platform/Track	*bee-nar-reeyo* **BINARIO**
Station	*statsee-yo-nay* **STAZIONE**
Taxi rank	*poss-tay-jo taxi* **POSTEGGIO TAXI**
Terminus	*capol-lee-naya* **CAPOLINEA**
Ticket office	*beelyetair-ree-ya* **BIGLIETTERIA**
Toilets	*toy-let-tay* **TOILETTE**

AI BINARI = TO PLATFORMS/TRACKS
ENTRATA = ENTRANCE
FERMATA A RICHIESTA = REQUEST STOP
FERMATA D'AUTOBUS = COMPULSORY STOP
USCITA = EXIT
VIETATO FUMARE = NO SMOKING

money & tipping: 50A

?

I	*ee-yo* **IO**	want	*vol-yo* **VOGLIO**
we	*noy* **NOI**	want	*vol-yar-mo* **VOGLIAMO**
you	*lay-ee* **LEI**	want	*vwar-lay* **VUOLE**
		have	*oh* **HO**
not	*non* **NON**	have	*abbee-yar-mo* **ABBIAMO**
no	*non* **NON**	have	*ah* **HA**
which	*kwar-lay* **QUALE**	is	*eh* **È**
where	*doh-vay* **DOVE**	are	*so-no* **SONO**
when	*kwan-doh* **QUANDO**	is there	*chay* **C'È**
what time	*kay or-ra* **CHE ORA**	can you	*pwoh* **PUÒ**

can I	*poss-o* **POSSO**
can I have	*poss-o ah-vair-ray* **POSSO AVERE**
can we	*possee-yar-mo* **POSSIAMO**
can we have	*possee-yar-mo ah-vair-ray* **POSSIAMO AVERE**
Arrive	*arree-var-ray* **ARRIVARE**
Change	*cambee-yar-ray* **CAMBIARE**
Depart	*par-teer-ray* **PARTIRE**
Get off	*shen-dairay* **SCENDERE**
Go	*an-dar-ray* **ANDARE**
Leave (things)	*la-shar-ray* **LASCIARE**
Reserve	*preno-tar-ray* **PRENOTARE**

		ticket	*beel-yet-toh* **BIGLIETTO**	sleeper	*vag-goh-nay let-toh* **VAGONE LETTO**
how long	*kwan-toh tem-po* **QUANTO TEMPO**	1st class	*pree-ma class-ay* **PRIMA CLASSE**	couchette	*koo-chet-ta* **CUCCETTA**
how many	*kwan-tee* **QUANTI**	2nd class	*sec-kon-da class-ay* **SECONDA CLASSE**	upper	*soopair-yor-ray* **SUPERIORE**
how often	*kwan-tay vol-tay* **QUANTE VOLTE**	single	*an-dar-ta* **ANDATA**	lower	*eenfair-yor-ray* **INFERIORE**
		return	*an-dar-ta eh ree-tor-no* **ANDATA E RITORNO**	seat	*poss-toh* **POSTO**
next to	*vee-chee-no ah* **VICINO A**	person	*pair-so-na* **PERSONA**	smoking	*foo-mar-ray* **FUMARE**
near	*vee-chee-no* **VICINO**	child/age	*bam-bee-no/et-ta* **BAMBINO ETÀ**	window	*fee-ness-tra* **FINESTRA**
here	*kwee* **QUI**				
there	*lar* **LÀ**			HOW MUCH IS (THAT)? *kwan-toh coss-ta* **QUANTO COSTA?**	
this	*kwess-toh* **QUESTO**				

these	*kwess-tee* **QUESTI**	at *al* **AL**	by *een* **IN**	for *pair* **PER**	from *dah* **DA**	in *dee* **DI**	on *soo* **SU**	to *ah* **A**

places: 24B money & tipping: 50A time: 60

English	Pronunciation / Italian		English	Pronunciation / Italian
journey	*vee-yar-jo* **VIAGGIO**		No.	*noo-mairo* **NUMERO**
			(express) Bus/Coach	*pool-man* **PULLMAN**
first	*pree-mo* **PRIMO**			
last	*ool-teemo* **ULTIMO**		Baggage car	*bagarlyee-yar-reeyo* **BAGAGLIAIO**
next	*pross-eemo* **PROSSIMO**		Carriage	*car-rot-sa* **CARROZZA**
			Dining car	*car-rot-sa reestor-ran-tay* **CARROZZA RISTORANTE**
early	*press-toh* **PRESTO**		Sleeping car	*vag-goh-nay let-toh* **VAGONE LETTO**
late	*een ree-tar-doh* **IN RITARDO**			
on time	*poontoo-ar-lay* **PUNTUALE**		meal	*pass-tee* **PASTI**
cancelled	*canchel-lar-ray* **CANCELLARE**		Morning call	*svay-leeya* **SVEGLIA**
			Tea/coffee	*tay/caf-fay* **TÉ CAFFÉ**
minutes	*mee-noo-tee* **MINUTI**			
hours	*or-ray* **ORE**		Bus/coach station	*statsee-yo-nay dee owtoh-boos* **STAZIONE DI AUTOBUS**
days	*jor-nee* **GIORNI**		Information	*eenfor-matsee-yo-nay* **INFORMAZIONE**
			Left luggage lockers	*arma-dee-yeto dep-poz-eetoh* **ARMADIETTO DEPOSITO**
train	*tray-no* **TRENO**		Left luggage office	*dep-poz-eetoh bag-gar-lyee* **DEPOSITO BAGAGLI**
lux express	*teh eh eh* **T E E**		Luggage	*bag-gar-lyee* **BAGAGLI**
express	*dee-re-tee-seemo* **DIRETTISSIMO**		Lost property	*oo-fee-cho od-jet-ee sma-ree-tee* **UFFICIO OGGETTI SMARRITI**
fast local	*dee-ret-oh* **DIRETTO**		Platform/Track	*bee-nar-reeyo* **BINARIO**
local	*lo-car-lay* **LOCALE**		Train station	*statsee-yo-nay* **STAZIONE**
			Ticket office	*beelyetair-ree-ya* **BIGLIETTERIA**
			Time table	*or-rar-reeyo fairovee-yar-reeyo* **ORARIO FERROVIARIO**
AI BINARI = TO PLATFORMS/TRACKS			Toilet	*toy-let-tay* **TOILETTE**
ENTRATA = ENTRANCE				
USCITA = EXIT			Waiting room	*sar-la das-pet-toh* **SALA D'ASPETTO**
VIETATO FUMARE = NO SMOKING				

?

I	*ee-yo* **IO**		
my	*eel mee-yo* **IL MIO**		
you	*lay-ee* **LEI**		
who	*kee* **CHI**		

not	*non* **NON**
no	*non* **NON**

which	*kwar-lay* **QUALE**
where	*doh-vay* **DOVE**
when	*kwan-doh* **QUANDO**

would like	*vor-ray-ee* **VORREI**	can you	*pwoh* **PUÒ**
want	*vwar-lay* **VUOLE**	Come back	*reepor-tar-ray* **RIPORTARE**
have	*oh* **HO**	Drive	*gwee-dar-ray* **GUIDARE**
have	*ah* **HA**	Explain	*spee-gar-ray* **SPIEGARE**
		Go	*an-dar-ray* **ANDARE**
is	*eh* **È**	Leave (vehicle)	*la-shar-ray* **LASCIARE**
are	*so-no* **SONO**	Pay	*pa-gar-ray* **PAGARE**
is there	*chay* **C'È**	Rent	*nolled-jar-ray* **NOLEGGIARE**
can I	*poss-o* **POSSO**	Ride	*an-dar-ray* **ANDARE**
can I have	*poss-o ah-vair-ray* **POSSO AVERE**	Show me	*mee moss-tree* **MI MOSTRI**

what time	*kay or-ra* **CHE ORA**	charge	*ta-ree-fa* **TARIFFA**	
		(full) insurance	*asseekoo-ratsee-yo-nay* **ASSICURAZIONE**	*(com-plet-tah)* **(COMPLETA)**
how far	*kwan-toh deess-tan-tay* **QUANTO DISTANTE**	total cost	*pret-so to-tar-lay* **PREZZO TOTALE**	
how long	*kwan-toh tem-po* **QUANTO TEMPO**	driving license	*pa-ten-tay* **PATENTE**	
how many	*kwan-tee* **QUANTI**	credit card	*car-ta dee cred-eetoh* **CARTA DI CREDITO**	
		deposit	*kowtsee-yo-nay* **CAUZIONE**	
near	*vee-chee-no* **VICINO**	identification	*eedentee-feekatsee-yo-nay* **IDENTIFICAZIONE**	
here	*kwee* **QUI**			
there	*lar* **LÀ**	HOW MUCH IS (THAT)?	*kwan-toh coss-ta* **QUANTO COSTA?**	
this	*kwess-toh* **QUESTO**			

these	*kwess-tee* **QUESTI**

and	at	by	for	from	in	to
ay **E**	*al* **AL**	*een* **IN**	*pair* **PER**	*dah* **DA**	*dee* **DI**	*ah* **A**

places: 24B   money: 50A   time: 60

small	*pee-kola* **PICCOLA**	Bicycle	*beechee-**klet**-tah* **BICICLETTA**
medium	*may-deeya* **MEDIA**	Car	*mak-keena* **MACCHINA**
large	***gran**-day* **GRANDE**	Moped	*motor-**ret**-tah* **MOTORETTA**
automatic	*owtoh-**mat**-eeka* **AUTOMATICA**	Motorcycle	*motochee-**klet**-ah* **MOTOCICLETTA**
manual	*ah **mar**-no* **A MANO**	Scooter	*scoo-ter* **SCOOTER**
		Sports car	*mak-keena spor-**tee**-va* **MACCHINA SPORTIVA**
cheaper	***may**-no **car**-ro* **MENO CARO**	Van	*for-**goh**-nay* **FURGONE**
better	*meel-**yor**-ray* **MIGLIORE**		
		how do . . . operate?	*koh-may foontsee-**yo**-na . . . ?* **COME FUNZIONA**
extra	*ex-tra* **EXTRA**	Brakes	*fray-nee* **FRENI**
included	*com-**pray**-so* **COMPRESO**	Gears	*mar-chay* **MARCE**
necessary	*nayches-**sar**-reeyo* **NECESSARIO**	Lights	*fan-**nar**-lee* **FANALI**
		Petrol/gas	*ben-**zee**-na* **BENZINA**
per	*al* **AL**	Reverse	*retro-**mar**-cha* **RETROMARCIA**
kilometer	*kee-**lo**-metro* **CHILOMETRO**	Tank (full)	*sairba-**toh**-eeyo (**pee**-yayno)* **SERBATOIO (PIENO)**
hour	*or-ra* **ORA**	Washers	*akwa pair tairjee-kree-**star**-lee* **ACQUA PER TERGICRISTALLI**
day	*jor-no* **GIORNO**	Wipers	*tairjee-kree-**star**-lee* **TERGICRISTALLI**
week	*settee-**mar**-na* **SETTIMANA**		
longer	*pee-yoo ah **loong**-go* **PIÙ A LUNGO**	Husband	*ma-**ree**-toh* **MARITO**
time	*or-ra* **ORA**	Wife	***mol**-yay* **MOGLIE**
		Son	***feel**-yo* **FIGLIO**
name	***no**-may* **NOME**	Daughter	***feel**-ya* **FIGLIA**
address	*eendee-**reet**-so* **INDIRIZZO**	Friend	*am-**mee**-ko* **AMICO**

?					
I	*ee-yo* **IO**	want	*vol-yo* **VOGLIO**	Change	*kambee-yar-ray* **CAMBIARE**
my	*eel mee-yo* **IL MIO**	want	*vwar-lay* **VUOLE**	Check	*con-tro-lee* **CONTROLLI**
you	*lay-ee* **LEI**			Clean	*poo-lee-ray* **PULIRE**
your	*eel soo-oh* **IL SUO**	have	*oh* **HO**	Fill up	*ree-em-pee-ray* **RIEMPIRE**
		have	*ah* **HA**	Get	*pren-dair-ray* **PRENDERE**
not	*non* **NON**			Go	*an-dar-ray* **ANDARE**
no	*non* **NON**	is	*eh* **È**	not Know	*non so* **NON SO**
		are	*so-no* **SONO**	Park	*par-ked-jar-ray* **PARCHEGGIARE**
which	*kwar-lay* **QUALE**			Pay	*pa-gar-ray* **PAGARE**
where	*doh-vay* **DOVE**	is there	*chay* **C'È**	not Possible	*eempos-see-beelay* **IMPOSSIBLE**
when	*kwan-doh* **QUANDO**	do you have	*ah-vet-tay* **AVETE**	will be Ready	*sa-rah pron-toh* **SARÀ PRONTO**
what	*koh-sa* **COSA**			Repair	*ree-par-rar-ray* **RIPARARE**
		can I	*poss-o* **POSSO**	See	*ved-dair-ray* **VEDERE**
what time	*kay or-ra* **CHE ORA**	can I have	*poss-o ah-vair-ray* **POSSO AVERE**	I'm Sorry	*mee deespee-yar-chay* **MI DISPIACE**
		can you	*pwoh* **PUÒ**	Stop	*fair-mar-ray* **FERMARE**

how long	*kwan-toh tem-po* **QUANTO TEMPO**				
how many	*kwan-tee* **QUANTI**				
		nearest	*pee-yoo vee-chee-no* **PIÙ VICINO**	open	*a-pair-toh* **APERTO**
near	*vee-chee-no* **VICINO**	receipt	*reechay-voo-ta* **RICEVUTA**	closed	*kee-oo-zo* **CHIUSO**
here	*kwee* **QUI**				
there	*lar* **LÀ**			HOW MUCH IS (THAT)?	*kwan-toh coss-ta* **QUANTO COSTA?**
this	*kwess-toh* **QUESTO**				
these	*kwess-tee* **QUESTI**				

	and	at	for	from	in	to	with
	ay **E**	*al* **AL**	*pair* **PER**	*dah* **DA**	*dee* **DI**	*ah* **A**	*con* **CON**

directions: 1   **breakdown & repair: 7**   **road signs: 9B**

BOARDER	*frontee-yair-rah* **FRONTIERA**		FILLING STATION	*deestreeboo-tor-ray* **DISTRIBUTORE**
Green card	*car-ta vair-day* **CARTA VERDE**		Car	*mak-keena* **MACCHINA**
Nothing to decl	*noo-la da deeka-rar-ray* **NULLA DA DICHIARARE**		Motorcycle	*motochee-klet-tah* **MOTOCICLETTA**
Passport	*passa-por-toh* **PASSAPORTO**		Oil	*ol-yo* **OLIO**
			Litres	*lee-tree* **LITRI**
POLICE	*poleet-see-ya/carabee-nyair-ree* **POLIZIA CARABINIERI**		Petrol/Gas	*ben-zee-na* **BENZINA**
Driver	*ow-tees-ta* **AUTISTA**		Regular/Super	*nor-ma-lay/soo-pair* **NORMALE SUPER**
Driving license	*pa-ten-tay* **PATENTE**			
Fine	*mool-ta* **MULTA**		Air (pressure)	*ar-reeya (pressee-yo-nay)* **ARIA (PRESSIONE)**
Insurance	*asseekoo-ratsee-yo-nay* **ASSICURAZIONE**		Distilled water	*akwa deestee-lar-tah* **ACQUA DISTILLATA**
Interpreter	*een-tair-pretay* **INTERPRETE**		Battery	*battair-ree-ya* **BATTERIA**
Km/hr	*kee-lo-metro ah-lor-ra* **KM ALL'ORA**		Puncture/Flat	*fora-too-ra* **FORATURA**
Police station	*statsee-yo-nay dee poleet-see-ya* **STAZIONE DI POLIZIA**		Tyre/Tire	*cam-maira darreya* **CAMERA D'ARIA**
Reg'n book	*lee-breto dee cheerco-latsee-yo-nay* **LIBRETTO DI CIRCOLAZIONE**		Water	*ak-wa* **ACQUA**
Sign	*sen-yar-lay* **SEGNALE**		Washers	*akwa pair tairjee-kree-star-lee* **ACQUA PER TERGICRISTALLI**
			Toilets	*toy-let-tay* **TOILETTE**
now	*a-dess-o* **ADESSO**		PARKING	*par-ked-jo* **PARCHEGGIO**
later	*pee-yoo tar-dee* **PIÙ TARDI**		Car park/Parking lot	*par-ked-jo* **PARCHEGGIO**
too fast	*trop-po for-tay* **TROPPO FORTE**		Parking disc	*dees-co or-rar-reeyo* **DISCO ORARIO**
not permitted	*veeyet-tar-toh* **VIETATO**		Parking lights	*la-shar-ray at-chay-zee* **LASCIARE ACCESI**
name	*no-may* **NOME**		Parking meter	*par-kee-maytro* **PARCHIMETRO**
address	*eendee-reet-so* **INDIRIZZO**		Small change	*speet-cho-lee* **SPICCIOLI**

money: 50A   **time: 60**   **conversion tables: 59A**

?

I	*ee-yo* **IO**
my	*eel mee-yo* **IL MIO**
you	*lay-ee* **LEI**
your	*eel soo-oh* **IL SUO**
not	*non* **NON**
no	*non* **NON**
which	*kwar-lay* **QUALE**
where	*doh-vay* **DOVE**
when	*kwan-doh* **QUANDO**
what	*koh-sa* **COSA**
what time	*kay or-ra* **CHE ORA**
how many	*kwan-tee* **QUANTI**
how much	*kwan-toh* **QUANTO**
how far	*kwan-toh deess-tan-tay* **QUANTO DISTANTE**
near	*vee-chee-no* **VICINO**
here	*kwee* **QUI**
there	*lar* **LÀ**
this	*kwess-toh* **QUESTO**
that	*kwel-lo* **QUELLO**

would like	*vor-ray-ee* **VORREI**
want	*vwar-lay* **VUOLE**
have	*oh* **HO**
have	*ah* **HA**
do you have	*ah-vet-tay* **AVETE**
is	*eh* **È**
are	*so-no* **SONO**
is there	*chay* **C'È**
can I	*poss-o* **POSSO**
can I have	*poss-o ah-vair-ray* **POSSO AVERE**
can you	*pwoh* **PUÒ**

Adjust	*ajoo-star-ray* **AGGIUSTARE**
Broken down	*een pan-nah* **IN PANNA**
Check	*con-tro-lee* **CONTROLLI**
Come	*pwoh ven-nee-ray* **PUÒ VENIRE**
Come back	*tor-nar-ray* **TORNARE**
will Cost	*costair-ra* **COSTERÀ**
Get	*pren-dair-ray* **PRENDERE**
give Lift	*dar-ray pas-sar-jo* **DARE PASSAGGIO**
Help	*ah-yoo-tar-ray* **AIUTARE**
Leave (vehicle)	*la-shar-ray* **LASCIARE**
will be Ready	*sar-rah pron-toh* **SARÀ PRONTO**
Repair	*reepa-rar-ray* **RIPARARE**
Replace	*sostee-too-wee-ray* **SOSTITUIRE**
give Tow	*try-no* **TRAINO**

itemised	*dettal-yar-toh* **DETTAGLIATO**
bill/check	*con-toh* **CONTO**
receipt	*reechay-voo-ta* **RICEVUTA**
nearest	*pee-yoo vee-chee-no* **PIÙ VICINO**
insurance	*asseekoo-ratsee-yo-nay* **ASSICURAZIONE**
cred'card	*car-ta dee cred-eetoh* **CARTA DI CREDITO**

HOW MUCH IS (THAT)? *kwan-toh coss-ta* **QUANTO COSTA?**

at	for	from	in	on	to	too
al **AL**	*pair* **PER**	*dah* **DA**	*een* **IN**	*soo* **SU**	*ah* **A**	*troppo* **TROPPO**

directions: 1   telephone: 48   money: 50A   time: 60

GUASTO & RIPARAZIONI
gwar-stoh ay reepa-ratsee-yo-nay

something	*qual-coh-sa* **QUALCOSA**	<u>SYMPTOMS</u>	*seen-toh-mee* **SINTOMI**
necessary	*netches-sair-reeyo* **NECESSARIO**	Broken	*rot-toh* **ROTTO**
temporarily	*provee-zor-reeyo* **PROVVISORIO**	Dirty	*spor-ko* **SPORCO**
very bad	*mol-toh cat-tee-vo* **MOLTO CATTIVO**	Dry	*seck-o* **SECCO**
new	*nwor-vo* **NUOVO**	Faulty	*gwarss-toh* **GUASTO**
		Frozen	*jel-lar-toh* **GELATO**
now	*a-dess-o* **ADESSO**	Jammed	*bloc-kar-toh* **BLOCCATO**
later	*pee-yoo tar-dee* **PIÙ TARDI**	Leaking	*fesoo-rar-toh* **FESSURATO**
sooner	*pee-yoo pres-toh* **PIÙ PRESTO**	Locked	*bloc-kar-toh* **BLOCCATO**
hours	*or-ray* **ORE**	Loose	*allen-tar-toh* **ALLENTATO**
days	*jor-nee* **GIORNI**	Misfiring	*see ah-chen-day ee-rairgo-la-men-tay* **SI ACCENDE IRREGOLAMENTE**
open	*a-pair-toh* **APERTO**	Noisy	*roomor-roh-so* **RUMOROSO**
closed	*kee-oo-zo* **CHIUSO**	Overheating	*soo-reescal-dar-toh* **SURRISCALDATO**
		Poor connection	*con-tat-o defet-toh-so* **CONTATTO DIFETTOSO**
Car	*mak-keena* **MACCHINA**	Slipping	*sheevo-lar-toh* **SCIVOLATO**
Garage	*ga-rarj* **GARAGE**	won't Start	non *par-tay* **NON PARTE**
Lubrication	*loobree-feekatsee-yo-nay* **LUBRIFICAZIONE**	vibrating	*vee-bra* **VIBRA**
Mechanic	*mek-kar-neeko* **MECCANICO**	not Working	non *foontsee-yo-na* **NON FUNZIONA**
Motorcycle	*motochee-klet-tah* **MOTOCICLETTA**	Worn	*consoo-mar-toh* **CONSUMATO**
Petrol/Gas Can	*bee-doh-nay pair ben-zee-na* **BIDONE PER BENZINA**		
Spare part	*pet-see dee ree-kam-beeyo* **PEZZI DI RICAMBIO**	name	*no-may* **NOME**
the Work	*eel la-vor-roh* **IL LAVORO**	address	*eendee-reet-so* **INDIRIZZO**

car/motorcycle parts: 8

English	Pronunciation / Italian		English	Pronunciation / Italian
Accelerator	*achellaira-tor-ray* **ACCCELERATORE**		Electrical system	*eempee-yan-toh el-let-reeco* **IMPIANTO ELETTRICO**
Air filter	*feel-tro del-lar-reeya* **FILTRO DELL'ARIA**		Engine	*mo-tor-ray* **MOTORE**
Alternator	*altairna-tor-ray* **ALTERNATORE**		Exhaust pipe	*too-boo dee scappa-men-toh* **TUBO DI SCAPPAMENTO**
Axle	*ass-ay* **ASSE**		Fan belt	*cheen-gheeya del venteela-tor-ray* **CINGHIA DEL VENTILATORE**
Battery	*battair-ree-ya* **BATTERIA**		Fuel pump	*pom-pa del carboo-ran-tay* **POMPA DEL CARBURANTE**
Bonnet	*cof-far-no* **COFANO**		Fuel tank	*sairbat-toh-eeyo della ben-zee-na* **SERBATOIO DELLA BENZINA**
Boot	*porta-bag-gar-lyee* **PORTABAGAGLI**		Fuse	*fee-zee-beelay* **FUSIBILE**
Brakes	*fray-nee* **FRENI**		Gear box	*scat-toh-la del cam-beeyo* **SCATOLA DEL CAMBIO**
Brake fluid	*floo-eedo pair ee fray-nee* **FLUIDO PER I FRENI**		Gears	*mar-chay* **MARCE**
Bulb	*lam-parday* **LAMPADE**		Gear lever/shift	*lay-va del cam-beeyo* **LEVA DEL CAMBIO**
Cable	*car-vo* **CAVO**		Globes	*lam-parday* **LAMPADE**
Carburettor	*carboo-rat-tor-ray* **CARBURATORE**		Handrake	*fray-no ah mar-no* **FRENO A MANO**
Choke	*val-voh-la del-lar-reeya* **VALVOLA DELL'ARIA**		Headlights	*far-ree antaire-yor-ree* **FARI ANTERIORI**
Clutch	*ee-ness-toh* **INNESTO**		Heating	*reescalda-men-toh* **RISCALDAMENTO**
Cooling system	*sees-tem-ma dee raffredda-men-toh* **SISTEMA DI RAFFREDDAMENTO**		Hood	*cof-farno* **COFANO**
			Horn	*clack-son* **CLACSON**
			Hose	*mannee-kot-toh* **MANICOTTO**
Cylindre	*chee-leen-dro* **CILINDRO**		Ign. system	*atchensee-yo-nay* **ACCENSIONE**
Dip/Dimmer switch	*commootat-tor-ray dellay loo-chee* **COMMUTATORE DELLE LUCI**		Indicator	*eendeecat-tor-ray* **INDICATORE**
			Inner tube	*cam-maira dar-reeya* **CAMERA D'ARIA**
Disc brake	*fray-no ah dees-ko* **FRENO A DISCO**		Jack	*kree-co* **CRICCO**
Distributor	*deestreeboo-tor-ray* **DISTRIBUTORE**		Levers	*lev-vay* **LEVE**
Dynamo	*dee-nammo* **DINAMO**		Lights	*loo-che* **LUCI**

brake light	*loo-chay del fray-no* **LUCE DEL FRENO**		Shock absorber	*ammorteetsa-tor-ray* **AMMORTIZZATORE**
hazard warning light	*sen-yar-lay loomee-no-so dee pair-ree-ko-lo* **SEGNALE LUMINOSO DI PERICOLO**		Silencer	*seelentseeya-tor-ray* **SILENZIATORE**
headlight	*far-ro antairee-yor-ray* **FARO ANTERIORE**		Spare part	*pet-so dee ree-cam-beeyo* **PEZZO DI RICAMBIO**
indicator light	*loo-chay eendeeca-tree-chay* **LUCE INDICATRICE**		Spark plug	*can-del-la* **CANDELA**
reversing light	*loo-chay della retro-mar-cha* **LUCE DELLA RETROMARCIA**		Speedometer	*tac-kee-metro* **TACHIMETRO**
sidelight	*loo-chay lattair-rar-lay* **LUCE LATERALE**		Starter motor	*motor-ree-no daveeya-men-toh* **MOTORINO D'AVVIAMENTO**
tail/rear light	*loo-chay postairee-yor-ray* **LUCE POSTERIORE**		Steering	*stairt-so* **STERZO**
			Suspension	*sospensee-yo-nay* **SOSPENSIONE**
			Transmission	*trazmeesee-yo-nay* **TRASMISSIONE**
Lubrication system	*sees-tem-ma dee loobree-feekatsee-yo-nay* **SISTEMA DI LUBRIFICAZIONE**		(automatic:	*(owtoh-mar-teeko)* **(AUTOMATICO)**
Mud guard	*para-fang-go* **PARAFANGO**		Trunk	*portabag-gar-lyee* **PORTABAGAGLI**
Muffler	*seelentseeya-tor-ray* **SILENZIATORE**		Turn indicator	*eendeecat-tor-ray* **INDICATORE**
Oil	*ol-yo* **OLIO**		Tyre/Tire	*coppair-toh-nay* **COPERTONE**
Oil filter	*feel-tro del-ol-yo* **FILTRO DELL'OLIO**		Wheel	*roo-wot-ta* **RUOTA**
Oil pressure gauge	*man-nom-metro del-ol-yo* **MANOMETRO DELL'OLIO**		Windscreen/ Windshield	*para-bret-sa* **parabrezza**
Petrol	*ben-zee-na* **BENZINA**		Washers	*ak-wa pair tairjee-krees-tar-lee* **ACQUA PER TERGICRISTALLI**
Radiator	*radeeya-tor-ray* **RADIATORE**		Wipers	*tairjee-krees-tar-lee* **TERGICRISTALLI**
Rear-view mirror	*speckee-yet-toh retrovee-zor-ray* **SPECCHIETTO RETROVISORE**			
Reflectors	*cattaree-fran-jen-tee* **CATARIFRANGENTI**		left	*see-neess-tra* **SINISTRA**
Seat	*sed-dee-lay* **SEDILE**		right	*dess-tra* **DESTRA**
Seat-belt	*cheen-tor-ra dee seekoo-ret-sa* **CINTURA DI SICUREZZA**		front	*da-van-tee* **DAVANTI**
			back	*dee-yay-tro* **DIETRO**

Italian to English section for the mechanic – overleaf: 9A

PEZZI	PARTS
ALBERO	shaft
ALBERO DI DISTRIBUZIONE	camshaft
ALBERO MOTORE	crankshaft
AMMORTIZZATORE	shock absorber
ASTE	stems
BASAMENTO	crankcase
BATTERIA	battery
BLOCCO DEL MOTORE	block
BOBINA	ignition coil
CANDELE	spark plugs
CARBURATORE	carburettor
CAVO	cable
CAVI	leads
CILINDRO	cylindre
CINGHIA DEL VENTILATORE	fanbelt
COLLEGAMENTO	connection
COMMUTATORE DELLE LUCI	dip (dimmer) switch
CONDENSATORE	condensor
CONTATTO	contact
CUSCINETTI	bearings
DENTI	teeth
DIAFRAMMA	diaphragm
DINAMO	dynamo (generator)
DISCO DELLA FRIZIONE	clutch plate
FASCE ELASTICHE	piston rings
FILTRO DELL'ARIA	air filter
FILTRO DELLA BENZINA	petrol (gas) filter
FILTRO DELL'OLIO	oil filter
FRENO	brake
FRIZIONE	clutch
GENERATORE	generator (dy'mo)
GIUNTO	joint
GIUNTO CARDANICO	universal joint
GUARNIZIONE	lining
GUARNIZIONE DELLA TESTA DEL CILINDRO	cylindre head gasket
IMPIANTO ELETTRICO	electrical system
MOLLE	springs
MOTORE	engine
MOTORINO D'AVVIA'TO	starter motor

PATTINI	shoes
PIANTONE DELLO STERZO	steering column
PISTONE	piston
POMPA DELL'ACQUA	water pump
POMPA DELLA BENZINA	fuel pump
POMPA D'INIEZIONE	injection pump
POMPA DELL'OLIO	oil pump
PUNTERIA	tappets
PUNTINE PLATINATE	points
RADIATORE	radiator
RUOTE	wheels
SCATOLA DELLO STERZO	steering box
SISTEMA DI RAFFREDDAMENTO	cooling system
SOSPENSIONE	suspension
SPAZZOLE	brushes
SPINTEROGENO	distributor
TAMBURO DEL FRENO	brake drum
TERMOSTATO	thermostat
TESTA DEL CILINDRO	cylindre head
TIRANTI TRANSVERSALI	track rod ends
TRANSMISSIONE	transmission
VALVOLA	valve
VENTILATORE	fan

SINTOMO	SYMPTOMS
BLOCCATO	jammed
CONSUMATO	worn
CONTATTO DIFETTOSO	bad connection
GELATO	frozen
NON STACCA BENE	slipping
PERDE	leaking
ROTTO	broken
SCIOLTO	loose
Secco	dry
SI ACCENDE IRR'TE	misfiring

COSE DA FARSI	SYMPTOMS
AGGIUSTARE	adjust
BILANCIARE	balance
CAMBIARE	change
CARICARE	charge
PULIRE	clean
SOSTITUIRE	replace
SPURGARE	bleed
STACCARE	strip down

ACCENDERE I FARI IN GALLERIA	Use headlights in tunnels
ACCOSTARE A SINISTRA	Keep left
ACCOSTARE A DESTRA	Keep right
ALTEZZA MASSIMA	Maximum height
ALT	Stop
AREA DI SERVIZIO	Service area
ATTENZIONE	Caution
AUTOSTRADA	Motorway/Freeway
BACINI PORTUALI	Docks
BENZINA	Petrol/Gas
CADUTA MASSI	Falling rocks
CARABINIERI	Police
CENTRO CITTÀ	City centre
CHIUSO	Closed
CIRCONVALLAZIONE	Ring road/belt highway
COMPLETO	Full
CORSIA D'EMERGENZA	Emergency parking
CURVE PER 2KM	Bends for 2km
DEVIAZIONE	Detour
DIVIETO DI SOSTA	No parking
DIVIETO DI SORPASSO	No overtaking
DOGANA	Customs
FINE	End
GALLERIA	Tunnel
LAVORI IN CORSO	Road works ahead
PAGAMENTO PEDAGGIO	Toll booths
PARCHEGGIO (ESAURITO)	Carpark/parking lot (full)
PARCHEGGIO SOCI	Reserved parking
PASSAGGIO A LIVELLO	Level/railroad crossing
PASSAGGIO SCOLARI	School crossing
PERICOLO	Danger
PERMANENTE CONTINUA	No parking
POLIZIA STRADALE	Highway police
RALLENTARE	Reduce speed
SEMAFORI SINCRONIZZATI	Synchronised traffic lights
SENSO UNICO	One way
SILENZIO	Silence
SOCCORSO A.C.I.	Motorists' emergency service
SORPASSO	Overtaking lane
TRAGHETTO	Ferry
TRANSITO CON CATENE	Tyre/tire chains required
USCITA	Exit
VICOLO CIECO	Dead end
VIETATO L'ACCESSO	No entry
VIGILI URBANI	City police
ZONA PEDONALE	Pedestrian area

ITALY

Overtaking by vehicles with trailers prohibited

Stop when meeting public transport bus on mountain road

stay in lane

Slow vehicle lane

SWITZERLAND

Semi-motorway

Parking disc compulsory

Postal vehicles have priority

Tunnel (lights compulsory)

(Flashing red light) level/railroad crossing

(Flashing lights) level/railroad crossing

?						
I	*ee-yo* **IO**	would like	*vor-ray-ee* **VORREI**	can I	*poss-o* **POSSO**	
my	*eel mee-yo* **IL MIO**	would like	*vor-ray-mo* **VORREMMO**	can I have	*poss-o ah-vair-ray* **POSSO AVERE**	
we	*noy* **NOI**	want	*vwar-lay* **VUOLE**	can you	*pwoh* **PUÒ**	
you	*lay-ee* **LEI**	have	*oh* **HO**			
		have	*abbee-yar-mo* **ABBIAMO**	Carry	*por-tar-ray* **PORTARE**	
not	*non* **NON**	have	*ah* **HA**	Depart	*par-teer-ray* **PARTIRE**	
no	*non* **NON**	do you have	*ah-vet-ray* **AVETE**	Pay	*pa-gar-ray* **PAGARE**	
				Reserve	*preno-tar-ray* **PRENOTARE**	
which	*kwar-lay* **QUALE**	is	*eh* **È**	Show me	*mee moss-tree* **MI MOSTRI**	
where	*doh-vay* **DOVE**	are	*so-no* **SONO**	Stay	*ress-tar-ray* **RESTARE**	
when	*kwan-doh* **QUANDO**	is there	*chay* **C'È**	Write	*scree-vairay* **SCRIVERE**	
what	*koh-sa* **COSA**					

what time	*kay or-ra* **CHE ORA**	per	*alla* **ALLA**	bill/check	*con-toh* **CONTO**
		night	*not-tay* **NOTTE**	includes	*com-pray-so* **COMPRESO**
how long	*kwan-toh tem-po* **QUANTO TEMPO**	week	*settee-mar-na* **SETTIMANA**	serv'ch	*coss-toh dee sair-veet-seeyo* **COSTO DI SERVIZIO**
how many	*kwan-tee* **QUANTI**	name	*no-may* **NOME**	taxes	*tass-say* **TASSE**
near	*vee-chee-no* **VICINO**	address	*eendee-reet-so* **INDIRIZZO**	cred'card	*car-ta dee cred-eetoh* **CARTA DI CREDITO**
here	*kwee* **QUI**	receipt	*reechay-voo-ta* **RICEVUTA**	checkout	*con-troh-lo par-tent-sah* **CONTROLLO PARTENZA**
there	*lar* **LÀ**				
this	*kwess-toh* **QUESTO**		HOW MUCH IS (THAT)?	*kwan-toh coss-ta* **QUANTO COSTA?**	
these	*kwess-tee* **QUESTI**				

at	for	from	in	of	until	with
al **AL**	*pair* **PER**	*dah* **DA**	*dee* **DI**	*dee* **DI**	*fee-no ah* **FINO A**	*con* **CON**

hotel enquiries & servies: 11   hotel problems: 12   family needs: 26

room	*cam-maira* **CAMERA**	Guest house	*pensee-yo-nay* **PENSIONE**
number	*noo-mairo* **NUMERO**	Hotel	*al-bair-go* **ALBERGO**
		Inn	*loc-kan-da* **LOCANDA**
cheap	*econ-nom-eeko* **ECONOMICO**	Motel	*mo-tel* **MOTEL**
good	*bwoh-no* **BUONO**		
high up	*een al-toh* **IN ALTO**	single room	*cam-maira seen-go-la* **CAMERA SINGOLA**
quiet	*trang-kwee-lo* **TRANQUILLO**	double room	*cam-maira matreemo-nee-yar-lay* **CAMERA MATRIMONIALE**
more	*pee-yoo* **PIÙ**	twin-bedded room	*cam-maira ah doo-ay let-tee* **CAMERA DUE LETTI**
alternative	*altairna-tee-va* **ALTERNATIVA**	cot/crib	*let-tee-no* **LETTINO**
extra	*ex-tra* **EXTRA**	bed	*let-toh* **LETTO**
near	*vee-chee-no* **VICINO**	bathroom	*ban-yo* **BAGNO**
front	*dah-van-tee* **DAVANTI**	shower	*dot-cha* **DOCCIA**
back	*dee-ett-ro* **DIETRO**	balcony	*tair-rat-so* **TERRAZZO**
		view	*veess-ta* **VISTA**
private	*pree-var-toh* **PRIVATO**	air-conditioning	*ar-reeya condeetseeyo-nar-ta* **ARIA CONDIZIONATA**
shared	*condee-vee-zo* **CONDIVISO**		
		bed & breakfast	*cam-maira ay colatsee-yo-nay* **CAMERA E COLAZIONE**
now	*a-dess-o* **ADESSO**	half-board	*met-sa pensee-yo-nay* **MEZZA PENSIONE**
later	*pee-yoo tar-dee* **PIÙ TARDI**	full-board	*pensee-yo-nay com-plet-ta* **PENSIONE COMPLETA**
probably	*proba-beel-men-tay* **PROBABILMENTE**		
quieter	*pee-yoo trang-kwee-lo* **PIÙ TRANQUILLO**	husband	*ma-ree-toh* **MARITO**
		wife	*mol-yay* **MOGLIE**
open	*a-pair-toh* **APERTO**	child	*bam-bee-no* **BAMBINO**
closed	*kee-oo-zo* **CHIUSO**	baby	*beem-bo* **BIMBO**

money & tipping: 50A   **time & days: 60**

?

English	Pronunciation	Italian
I	*ee-yo*	**IO**
my	*eel mee-yo*	**IL MIO**
our	*noss-tro*	**NOSTRO**
you	*lay-ee*	**LEI**
your	*eel soo-oh*	**IL SUO**
not	*non*	**NON**
no	*non*	**NON**
which	*kwar-lay*	**QUALE**
where	*doh-vay*	**DOVE**
when	*kwan-doh*	**QUANDO**

English	Pronunciation	Italian
would like	*vor-ray-ee*	**VORREI**
want	*vwar-lay*	**VUOLE**
have	*oh*	**HO**
have	*ah*	**HA**
do you have	*ah-vet-tay*	**AVETE**
is	*eh*	**È**
are	*so-no*	**SONO**
is there	*chay*	**C'È**
can I	*poss-o*	**POSSO**
can I have	*poss-o ah-vair-ray*	**POSSO AVERE**
can you	*pwoh*	**PUÒ**

English	Pronunciation	Italian
Carry	*por-tar-ray*	**PORTARE**
Call me	*kee-yar-mee*	**MI CHIAMI**
Change	*cambee-yar-ray*	**CAMBIARE**
Go	*an-dar-ray*	**ANDARE**
Leave (things)	*la-shar-ray*	**LASCIARE**
Order	*ordee-nar-ray*	**ORDINARE**
Pay	*pa-gar-ray*	**PAGARE**
Post	*eemposs-tar-ray*	**IMPOSTARE**
will be ready	*sar-rah pron-toh*	**SARÀ PRONTO**
Show me	*mee moss-treee*	**MI MOSTRI**
will Take	*chee vwar-lay*	**CI VUOLE**
Telephone	*telefon-ar-ray*	**TELEFONARE**

English	Pronunciation	Italian
what time	*kay or-ra*	**CHE ORA**
how long	*kwan-toh tem-po*	**QUANTO TEMPO**
how many	*kwan-tee*	**QUANTI**

English	Pronunciation	Italian
hours	*or-ray*	**ORE**
days	*jor-nee*	**GIORNI**
today	*od-jee*	**OGGI**

English	Pronunciation	Italian
tomorrow	*dom-mar-nee*	**DOMANI**
morning	*mat-tee-no*	**MATTINO**
afternoon	*pommair-reed-jo*	**POMERIGGIO**

English	Pronunciation	Italian
near	*vee-chee-no*	**VICINO**
here	*kwee*	**QUI**
there	*lar*	**LÀ**
this	*kwess-toh*	**QUESTO**
these	*kwess-tee*	**QUESTI**

English	Pronunciation	Italian
JUST A MOMENT!	*oon ar-teemo*	**UN ATTIMO**
COME IN!	*ah-van-tee*	**AVANTI!**
HOW MUCH IS (THAT)?	*kwan-toh coss-ta*	**QUANTO COSTA?**

	at	by	for	from	in	of	to
	al	*een*	*pair*	*dah*	*een*	*dee*	*ah*
	AL	**IN**	**PER**	**DA**	**IN**	**DI**	**A**

hotel problems: 12   family needs: 26   drinks: 31B & 32A   snacks: 32B

name	*no-may* **NOME**	breakfast	*collatsee-yo-nay* **COLAZIONE**
room	*cam-mairra* **CAMERA**	lunch	*prant-so* **PRANZO**
number	*noo-mairo* **NUMERO**	dinner	*chay-na* **CENA**
		snack	*spoon-tee-no* **SPUNTINO**
now	*a-dess-o* **ADESSO**	drink	*bee-beeta* **BIBITA**
later	*pee-yoo tar-dee* **PIÙ TARDI**		
soon	*press-toh* **PRESTO**		
		Car	*mak-keena* **MACCHINA**
open	*a-pair-toh* **APERTO**	Front door	*por-ta antairree-yor-ray* **PORTA ANTERIORE**
closed	*kee-oo-zo* **CHIUSO**	Key	*kee-yar-vay* **CHIAVE**
		Luggage	*bag-garl-yee* **BAGAGLI**
Bar	*bar* **BAR**	Mail	*poss-ta* **POSTA**
Creche	*as-see-lo* **ASILO**	Message	*mess-sar-jo* **MESSAGGIO**
Dining room	*sar-la dah prant-so* **SALA DA PRANZO**	Money	*den-nar-ro* **DENARO**
Hairdresser	*parrookee-yair-ray* **PARRUCCHIERE**	Morning call	*svay-leeya* **SVEGLIA**
Left luggage	*dep-poz-eetoh bag-garl-yee* **DEPOSITO BAGAGLI**	Security Safe	*cassa-for-tay* **CASSAFORTE**
Lounge	*sar-la* **SALA**	Taxi	*taxi* **TAXI**
Reception	*oo-fee-cho reechayvee-men-toh* **UFFICIO RICEVIMENTO**	Valuables	*od-jet-tee pret-see-yo-see* **OGGETTI PREZIOSI**
Toilet	*toy-let-tay* **TOILETTE**	Trav' cheques/checks	*trev-ooluz sheck* **TRAVELLERS' CHEQUE**
Manager	*dee-ret-tor-ray* **DIRETTORE**	Clothes	*vess-tee-tee* **VESTITI**
Maid	*camairree-yair-ra* **CAMERIERA**	Drycleaned	*poo-lee-toh ah sec-ko* **PULITO A SECCO**
Porter	*portee-yair-ray* **PORTIERE**	Ironed	*stee-rar-toh* **STIRATO**
Room service	*val-let-toh* **VALLETTO**	Laundered	*lav-var-toh* **LAVATO**

ining room: 27   telephone: 48   tipping: 50A   cleaners: 50B   time: 60

?				
I	*ee-yo* **IO**	would like	*vor-ray-ee* **VORREI**	can I	*poss-o* **POSSO**
my	*eel mee-yo* **IL MIO**	want	*vwar-lay* **VUOLE**	can I have	*poss-o ah-vair-ray* **POSSO AVERE**
our	*noss-tro* **NOSTRO**	have	*oh* **HO**	Clean	*poo-lee-ray* **PULIRE**
you	*lay-ee* **LEI**	have	*ah* **HA**	Change	*cambee-yar-ray* **CAMBIARE**
your	*eel soo-oh* **IL SUO**	do you have	*ah-vet-tay* **AVETE**	Come	*ven-nee-ray* **VENIRE**
				Leave (things)	*la-shar-ray* **LASCIARE**
not	*non* **NON**	is	*eh* **È**	Lost	*pair-doo-toh* **PERDUTO**
no	*non* **NON**	are	*so-no* **SONO**	Make up	*far-ray* **FARE**
		is there	*chay* **C'È**	Need	*bee-son-yo* **BISOGNO**
which	*kwar-lay* **QUALE**	can you	*pwoh* **PUÒ**	Show me	*mee moss-stree* **MI MOSTRI**
where	*doh-vay* **DOVE**				
what	*koh-sa* **COSA**				
when	*kwan-doh* **QUANDO**	maid	*cammairee-yair-ra* **CAMERIERA**	room	*cam-maira* **CAMERA**
		porter	*cammairee-yair-ray* **CAMERIERE**	number	*noo-mairo* **NUMERO**
what time	*kay or-ra* **CHE ORA**	room service	*val-let-toh* **VALLETTO**	reception	*oo-fee-cheeo reechayvee-men-toh* **UFFICIO RICEVIMENTO**
how many	*kwan-tee* **QUANTI**				

JUST A MOMENT! *oon ar-teemo* **UN ATTIMO!**

COME IN *a-van-tee* **AVANTI**

near	*vee-chee-no* **VICINO**
here	*kwee* **QUI**
there	*lar* **LÀ**
this	*kwess-toh* **QUESTO**
these	*kwess-tee* **QUESTI**

SUONARE PER SERVIZIO = RING FOR SERVICE

and	by	for	in	on	to	too
ay **E**	*een* **IN**	*pair* **PER**	*een* **IN**	*soo* **SU**	*ah* **A**	*trop-po* **TROPPO**

hotel services: 11   family needs: 26   telephone: 48   time: 60

English	Pronunciation / Italian		English	Pronunciation / Italian
dirty	*spor-ko* **SPORCO**		Heating	*reescalda-men-toh* **RISCALDAMENTO**
noisy	*roomor-roh-so* **RUMOROSO**		Key	*kee-yar-vay* **CHIAVE**
not working	*non foontsee-yo-na* **NON FUNZIONA**		Laundry	*boo-car-toh* **BUCATO**
broken	*rot-toh* **ROTTO**		Lift	*ashen-sor-ray* **ASCENSORE**
			Light bulb/globe	*lampa-dee-na* **LAMPADINA**
hot	*cal-doh* **CALDO**	cold *fray-doh* **FREDDO**	Lock	*saira-too-ra* **SERRATURA**
on	*a-chess-so* **ACCESSO**	off *spen-toh* **SPENTO**	Note paper	*car-ta dah let-tairay* **CARTA DA LETTERE**
some	*kwal-kay* **QUALCHE**		Pillow	*gwanchee-yar-lay* **GUANCIALE**
extra	*ex-tra* **EXTRA**		Pillowcase	*fed-daira* **FEDERA**
fresh	*fray-sko* **FRESCO**		Plug (basin)	*tar-po* **TAPPO**
open	*a-pair-toh* **APERTO**		Razor socket	*pray-sa pair eel ra-zoy-eeyo* **PRESA PER IL RASOIO**
closed	*kee-oo-zo* **CHIUSO**		Sheet	*lent-swo-lo* **LENZUOLO**
Air cond'ning	*ar-reeya condeetseeyo-nar-ta* **ARIA CONDIZIONATA**		Soap	*sap-po-nay* **SAPONE**
Ashtray	*porta-chay-nairay* **PORTACENERE**		Shower	*dot-cha* **DOCCIA**
Bath	*ban-yo* **BAGNO**		Toilet	*toy-lett-tay* **TOILETTE**
Bed	*let-toh* **LETTO**		Toilet paper	*car-ta ee-jee-neeka* **CARTA IGIENICA**
Blanket	*cop-pairta* **COPERTA**		Towel	*ashoogar-mar-no* **ASCIUGAMANO**
Coat hangers	*attaca-par-nee* **ATTACCAPANNI**		Television	*telayvee-zor-ray* **TELEVISORE**
Drinking water	*ak-wa pot-tar-beelay* **ACQUA POTABILE**		Ventilator	*venteelatsee-yo-nay* **VENTILAZIONE**
Duvet	*peeyoo-moh-nay* **PIUMONE**		Voltage	*vol-tar-jo (220/110)* **VOLTAGGIO**
Elevator	*ashen-sor-ray* **ASCENSORE**		Wash basin	*lavan-dee-no* **LAVANDINO**
Electricity	*elletreechee-ta* **ELETTRICITÀ**		Water	*ak-wa* **ACQUA**
			Window	*fee-ness-tra* **FINESTRA**

tipping: 50A

?	I	*ee-yo* **IO**	would like	*vor-ray-ee* **VORREI**		can I	*poss-o* **POSSO**
	my	*eel mee-yo* **IL MIO**	want	*vwar-lay* **VUOLE**		can I have	*poss-o ah-vair-ray* **POSSO AVERE**
	you	*lay-ee* **LEI**	have	*oh* **HO**		Fix	*seestay-mar-ray* **SISTEMARE**
	your	*eel soo-oh* **IL SUO**	have	*ah* **HA**		Need	*bee-son-yo* **BISOGNO**
						Park	*par-ked-jar-ray* **PARCHEGGIARE**
	not	*non* **NON**	is	*eh* **È**		Pay	*pa-gar-ray* **PAGARE**
	no	*non* **NON**	are	*so-no* **SONO**		Rent	*noled-jar-ray* **NOLEGGIARE**
			is there	*chay* **C'È**		Show me	*mee moss-tree* **MI MOSTRI**
	which	*kwar-lay* **QUALE**	can you	*pwoh* **PUÒ**		Use	*oo-zar-ray* **USARE**

where	*doh-vay*	**DOVE**
what	*koh-sa*	**COSA**
when	*kwan-doh*	**QUANDO**

			booking	*prenotatsee-yo-nay* **PRENOTAZIONE**		dirty	*spor-ko* **SPORCO**
			deposit	*dep-poz-eetoh* **DEPOSITO**		broken	*rot-toh* **ROTTO**
what time	*kay or-ra* **CHE ORA**		service	*sair-veet-seeyo* **SERVIZIO**		not working	*non foontsee-yo-na* **NON FUNZIONA**
			included	*com-pray-so* **COMPRESO**		extra	*ex-tra* **EXTRA**
how long	*kwan-toh tem-po* **QUANTO TEMPO**		receipt	*reechay-voo-ta* **RICEVUTA**		better	*meel-yor-ray* **MIGLIORE**
how many	*kwan-tee* **QUANTI**		check out	*con-troh-lo par-tent-sa* **CONTROLLO PARTENZA**	furnished	*ammobeelee-yar-toh* **AMMOBILIATO**
			name	*no-may* **NOME**		tel no.	*noo-mairo dee tel-lef-onno* **NUMERO DI**
near	*vee-chee-no* **VICINO**		address	*eendee-reet-so* **INDIRIZZO**			**TELEFONO**
here	*kwee* **QUI**						
there	*lar* **LÀ**			HOW MUCH IS (THAT)?	*kwan-toh coss-ta* **QUANTO COSTA?**		
this	*kwess-toh* **QUESTO**						

	and	by	for	from	in	on	to
these	*ay*	*een*	*pair*	*dah*	*een*	*soo*	*ah*
kwess-tee **QUESTI**	**E**	**IN**	**PER**	**DA**	**IN**	**SU**	**A**

bathroom	*ban-yo* **BAGNO**		Curtains	*ten-day* **TENDE**
bedroom	*cam-maira dah let-toh* **CAMERA DA LETTO**		Door	*por-ta* **PORTA**
kitchen	*koo-chee-na* **CUCINA**		Electricity	*elletree-chee-ta* **ELETTRICITÀ**
living room	*soj-jor-no* **SOGGIORNO**		Fuses	*foo-zee-beelee* **FUSIBILI**
garden	*jar-dee-no* **GIARDINO**		Gas	*gas* **GAS**
			Heating	*reescalda-men-toh* **RISCALDAMENTO**
car	*mak-keena* **MACCHINA**		Keys	*kee-yar-vay* **CHIAVE**
road	*strar-da* **STRADA**		Lamp	*lam-parda* **LAMPADA**
garage	*ga-rarj* **GARAGE**		Light bulb/globe	*lampa-dee-na* **LAMPADINA**
grocer shop	*drog-air-ree-ya* **DROGHERIA**		Lock	*saira-too-ra* **SERRATURA**
			Refrigerator	*freegor-ree-fairo* **FRIGORIFERO**
bed	*let-toh* **LETTO**		Shower	*dot-cha* **DOCCIA**
bedding	*beeyankair-ree-ya* **BIANCHERIA**		Sink	*ak-way-yo* **ACQUAIO**
blanket	*cop-pair-ta* **COPERTA**		Table	*tar-volo* **TAVOLO**
duvet	*peeyoo-moh-nay* **PIUMONE**		Tap	*roobee-net-toh* **RUBINETTO**
pillow	*gwanchee-yar-lay* **GUANCIALE**		Telephone	*tel-lef-onno* **TELEFONO**
pillow case	*fed-daira* **FEDERA**		Television	*televee-zor-ray* **TELEVISORE**
sheet	*lent-swo-lo* **LENZUOLO**		Toilet	*toy-let-tay* **TOILETTE**
			Vacuum cleaner	*as-pee-ra-pol-vairay* **ASPIRAPOLVERE**
how operates?	*koh-may foontsee-yo-na* **COME FUNZIONA?**		Wash basin	*lavan-dee-no* **LAVANDINO**
			(drinking) Water	*ak-wa pot-tar-beelay* **ACQUA POTABILE**
Bath	*ban-yo* **BAGNO**		Water heater	*scalda-ban-yo* **SCALDABAGNO**
Chair	*sed-deeya* **SEDIA**		Window	*fee-ness-tra* **FINESTRA**
Cooker	*koo-chee-na* **CUCINA**			

household utensils: 16A

?

I	*ee-yo* **IO**	would like	*vor-ray-ee* **VORREI**	Buy *com-prar-ray* **COMPRARE**
my	*eel mee-yo* **IL MIO**	would like	*vor-ray-mo* **VORREMMO**	Clean *poo-lee-ray* **PULIRE**
we	*noy* **NOI**	want	*vwar-lay* **VUOLE**	Come back *tor-nar-ray* **TORNARE**
our	*noss-tro* **NOSTRO**			Cook *kwo-chairay* **CUOCERE**
you	*lay-ee* **LEI**	have	*oh* **HO**	Dry *ashoo-gar-ray* **ASCIUGARE**
		have	*abbee-yar-mo* **ABBIAMO**	Go *an-dar-ray* **ANDARE**
not	*non* **NON**	have	*ah* **HA**	Join *ees-cree-vairay* **ISCRIVERE**
no	*non* **NON**	do you have	*ah-vet-tay* **AVETE**	Leave (things) *la-shar-ray* **LASCIARE**
		is	*eh* **È**	Pay *pa-gar-ray* **PAGARE**
which	*kwar-lay* **QUALE**	are	*so-no* **SONO**	Rent *nolled-jar-ray* **NOLEGGIARE**
where	*doh-vay* **DOVE**	is there	*chay* **C'È**	Reserve *preno-tar-ray* **PRENOTARE**
when	*kwan-doh* **QUANDO**			Stay *ress-tar-ray* **RESTARE**
		can I	*poss-o* **POSSO**	Tidy *met-tair-ray een or-dee-nay* **METTERE IN ORDINE**
what time	*kay or-ra* **CHE ORA**	can I have	*poss-o ah-vair-ray* **POSSO AVERE**	
		can we	*possee-yar-mo* **POSSIAMO**	Wash *la-var-ray* **LAVARE**

how long	*kwan-toh tem-po* **QUANTO TEMPO**		
how many	*kwan-tee* **QUANTI**	per *al* **AL**	memb' card *tess-saira* **TESSERA**
		night *not-tay* **NOTTE**	name *no-may* **NOME**
near	*vee-chee-no* **VICINO**	week *settee-mar-na* **SETTIMANA**	address *eendee-reet-so* **INDIRIZZO**
here	*kwee* **QUI**		
there	*lar* **LÀ**	HOW MUCH IS (THAT)? *kwan-toh* **QUANTO COSTA?**	
this	*kwess-toh* **QUESTO**		
these	*kwess-tee* **QUESTI**		

	at	for	from	in	of	to	with
	al **AL**	*pair* **PER**	*dah* **DA**	*een* **IN**	*dee* **DI**	*ah* **A**	*con* **CON**

soft drinks: 31B   snacks: 32B   food: 33   money: 50A

early	*press-toh* **PRESTO**		number	*noo-mairo* **NUMERO**
now	*a-dess-o* **ADESSO**			
later	*pee-yoo tar-dee* **PIÙ TARDI**		Bed	*let-toh* **LETTO**
			Dormitory	*dormee-tor-reeyo* **DORMITORIO**
next	*pross-seemo* **PROSSIMO**		Dining room	*sar-la dah prant-so* **SALA DA PRANZO**
near	*vee-chee-no* **VICINO**		Kitchen	*koo-chee-na* **CUCINA**
another	*oon al-tro* **UN ALTRO**		Lounge	*sar-la* **SALA**
			Shower	*dot-cha* **DOCCIA**
before	*pree-ma* **PRIMA**		Toilet	*toy-let-tay* **TOILETTE**
after	*dor-po* **DOPO**		(mens'/womens')	*(woh-meenee/don-nay)* **(UOMINI DONNE)**
on	*at-chay-so* **ACCESO**			
off	*spen-toh* **SPENTO**		Blanket	*cop-pair-ta* **COPERTA**
			Clothes	*vess-tee-tee* **VESTITI**
open	*a-pair-toh* **APERTO**		Duty (job)	*dor-vair-ray* **DOVERE**
closed	*kee-oo-zo* **CHIUSO**		Entrance door	*een-gray-so* **INGRESSO**
all day	*too-toh eel jor-no* **TUTTO IL GIORNO**		Groceries	*jay-nairee aleemen-tar-ree* **GENERI ALIMENTARI**
tonight	*sta-not-tay* **STANOTTE**		Key	*kee-yar-vay* **CHIAVE**
tomorrow	*dom-mar-nee* **DOMANI**		Lights	*loo-chee* **LUCI**
morning	*mat-tee-no* **MATTINO**		Locker	*arma-dee-yet-toh* **ARMADIETTO**
evening	*sair-ra* **SERA**		Meals	*pas-tee* **PASTI**
			Security safe	*cassa-for-tay* **CASSAFORTE**
breakfast	*collatsee-yo-nay* **COLAZIONE**		Sleeping bag	*sac-ko ah pair-lo* **SACCO A PELO**
lunch	*prant-so* **PRANZO**		Sleeping sheet	*sac-ko ah lent-swo-lo* **SACCO A LENZUOLO**
dinner	*chay-na* **CENA**		Valuables	*od-jet-tee pret-see-yo-see* **OGGETTI PREZIOSI**

---

time: 60   **furniture: 13B**   **household utensils: 16A**

? I *ee-yo* **IO**

my *eel mee-yo* **IL MIO**

we *noy* **NOI**

our *noss-tro* **NOSTRO**

you *lay-ee* **LEI**

not *non* **NON**

no *non* **NON**

which *kwar-lay* **QUALE**

where *doh-vay* **DOVE**

when *kwan-doh* **QUANDO**

what time *kay or-ra* **CHE ORA**

how long *kwan-toh tem-po* **QUANTO TEMPO**

how many *kwan-tee* **QUANTI**

near *vee-chee-no* **VICINO**

here *kwee* **QUI**

there *lar* **LÀ**

this *kwess-toh* **QUESTO**

these *kwess-tee* **QUESTI**

---

would like *vor-ray-ee* **VORREI**

would like *vor-ray-mo* **VORREMMO**

want *vwar-lay* **VUOLE**

have *oh* **HO**

have *abbee-yar-mo* **ABBIAMO**

have *ah* **HA**

do you have *ah-vet-tay* **AVETE**

is *eh* **È**

are *so-no* **SONO**

is there *chay* **C'È**

---

can I *poss-o* **POSSO**

can we *possee-yar-mo* **POSSIAMO**

Buy *com-prar-ray* **COMPRARE**

Camp *cam-ped-jar-ray* **CAMPEGGIARE**

Come back *tor-nar-ray* **TORNARE**

Depart *par-teer-ray* **PARTIRE**

Leave (things) *la-shar-ray* **LASCIARE**

Light (fire) *at-chen-dairay* **ACCENDERE**

Park *par-ked-jar-ray* **PARCHEGGIARE**

Pitch *met-airay* **METTERE**

Stay *ress-tar-ray* **RESTARE**

Wash *la-var-ray* **LAVARE**

---

per *al* **AL**

night *not-tay* **NOTTE**

person *pair-so-na* **PERSONA**

tent *ten-da* **TENDA**

vehicle *vay-co-lo* **VEICOLO**

nearest *pee-yoo vee-chee-no* **PIÙ VICINO**

name *no-may* **NOME**

address *eendee-reet-so* **INDIRIZZO**

the charge *eel pret-so* **IL PREZZO**

receipt *reechay-voo-ta* **RICEVUTA**

HOW MUCH IS (THAT)? *kwan-toh* **QUANTO COSTA?**

and	by	for	from	in	on	to
ay	*een*	*pair*	*dah*	*een*	*soo*	*ah*
E	**IN**	**PER**	**DA**	**IN**	**SU**	**A**

---

camping equipment: 16A   countryside: 16B   food: 33   money: 50A

open	*a-**pair**-toh* **APERTO**	Camping ground	*cam-**ped**-jo* **CAMPEGGIO**
closed	*kee-**oo**-zo* **CHIUSO**	Facilities	*fatcheelee-tatsee-**yo**-nee* **FACILITAZIONI**
all day	*too-toh eel jor-no* **TUTTO IL GIORNO**	Field	*cam-po* **CAMPO**
		Gate	*can-**chel**-lo* **CANCELLO**
before	*pree-ma* **PRIMA**	Shop	*spat-cho* **SPACCIO**
after	*dor-po* **DOPO**	Showers	*dot-chee* **DOCCIE**
early	*press-toh* **PRESTO**	Site	*poss-toh* **POSTO**
late	*tar-dee* **TARDI**	Toilets	*toy-**let**-tay* **TOILETTE**
		Washroom	*ban-yo* **BAGNO**
near	*vee-**chee**-no* **VICINO**		
anywhere	*dappair-**too**-toh* **DAPPERTUTTO**		
away from	*deess-**tan**-tay dah* **DISTANTE DA**		
		Dishes	*pee-**yar**-tee* **PIATTI**
noisy	*roomor-**roh**-so* **RUMOROSO**	Drinking water	*ak-wa pot-**tar**-beelay* **ACQUA POTABILE**
quiet	*trang-**kwee**-lo* **TRANQUILLO**	Farmer	*fat-**tor**-ray* **FATTORE**
sheltered	*reepa-**rar**-toh* **RIPARATO**	Food	*chee-bo* **CIBO**
		Fire	*fwock-oh* **FUOCO**
alternative	*altairna-**tee**-va* **ALTERNATIVA**	Security Safe	*cassa-**for**-tay* **CASSAFORTE**
more	*pee-yoo* **PIÙ**	Tent	*ten-da* **TENDA**
less	*may-no* **MENO**	Valuables	*od-**jet**-tee pretsee-**yo**-see* **OGGETTI PREZIOSI**
		Water	*ak-wa* **ACQUA**
bicycle	*beechee-**klet**-ta* **BICICLETTA**		
car	*mak-keena* **MACCHINA**		
caravan/trailer	*roo-lot* **ROULOTTE**		
motorcycle	*motochee-**klet**-ta* **MOTOCICLETTA**		

VIETATO CAMPEGGIARE = NO CAMPING
ROULOTTE VIETATE = NO CARAVANS/TRAILERS
VIETATO L'INGRESSO = NO TRESSPASSING

time: 60

lightweight	*lay-**jair**-ro* **LEGGERO**	Guy line	*tee-**ran**-tay* **TIRANTE**
plastic	*plass-teeka* **PLASTICA**	Knife	*col-**tel**-lo* **COLTELLO**
stainless steel	*at-**chee**-yo eenossee-**dar**-beelay* **ACCIAIO INOSSIDABILE**	Lamp	*lam-parda* **LAMPADA**
		Mallet	*mat-sa* **MAZZA**
Air mattress	*lie lo* **LILO**	Matches	*feeya-**mee**-fairee* **FIAMMIFERI**
Air pump	*pom-pa* **POMPA**	Mosquito net	*zanzaree-**yair**-ra* **ZANZARIERA**
Back pack	*tsah-**yee**-no* **ZAINO**	Paraffin	*kairo-**say**-nay* **KEROSENE**
Bottle opener	*apreebot-**teel**-ya* **APRIBOTTIGLIA**	Pen knife	*coltel-**leeno*** **COLTELLINO**
Brush	*spat-so-la* **SPAZZOLA**	Plate	*pee-ya-toh* **PIATTO**
Bucket	*seck-eeyo* **SECCHIO**	Rope	*foo-nay* **FUNE**
Butane gas	*gaz boo-**tar**-no* **GAS BUTANO**	Rucksack	*tsah-**yee**-no* **ZAINO**
Camp bed	*bran-**dee**-na* **BRANDINA**	Saucepan	*cassair-**woh**-la* **CASSERUOLA**
Camp chair	*sedjo-**lee**-no* **SEGGIOLINO**	Sleeping bag	*sac-ko ah **pair**-lo* **SACCO A PELO**
Can opener	*apree-scat-toh-lay* **APRISCATOLE**	Space blanket	*cop-**pair**-ta spatsee-**yar**-lay* **COPERTA SPAZIALE**
Compass	*boos-so-la* **BUSSOLA**	Spoon	*kookee-**ya**-oh* **CUCCHIAIO**
Corkscrew	*cava-**tap**-pee* **CAVATAPPI**	Stove	*stoo-fa* **STUFA**
Cup	*tat-sa* **TAZZA**	Tent	*ten-da* **TENDA**
Dehydrated food	*chee-bee sec-kee* **CIBI SECCHI**	Tent peg	*pee-ket-toh* **PICCHETTO**
First aid kit	*cas-et-ta del pron-to soc-**kor**-so* **CASSETTA DEL PRONTO SOCCORSO**	Tent pole	*par-lo* **PALO**
Flashlight	*pee-la* **PILA**	Tin opener	*apree-scat-toh-lay* **APRISCATOLE**
Fork	*for-**ket**-ta* **FORCHETTA**	Thermos flask	*tair-mos* **THERMOS**
Frying pan	*pa-**del**-la* **PADELLA**	Torch	*pee-la* **PILA**
Ground sheet	*tel-lo pair eel tair-**ray**-no* **TELO PER IL TERRENO**	Water carrier	*bee-**doh**-nay pair lak-wa* **BIDONE PER L'ACQUA**

?

can I	*poss-o*	**POSSO**
can we	*possee-yar-mo*	**POSSIAMO**
is	*eh*	**È**
are	*so-no*	**SONO**
is there	*chay*	**C'È**
Climb	*scal-lar-ray*	**SCALARE**
Cross	*attravair-sar-ray*	**ATTRAVERSARE**
Go	*an-dar-ray*	**ANDARE**
have Lift	*a-vair-ray oon pass-ar-jo*	**AVERE UN PASSAGGIO**
Swim	*noo-oh-tar-ray*	**NUOTARE**
not	*non*	**NON**
which	*kwar-lay*	**QUALE**
what	*koh-sa*	**COSA**
near	*vee-chee-no*	**VICINO**
here	*kwee*	**QUI**
there	*lar*	**LÀ**
this	*kwess-toh*	**QUESTO**
that	*kwel-lo*	**QUELLO**

over	*sop-ra*	**SOPRA**
under	*sot-toh*	**SOTTO**
name of	*no-may dee*	**NOME DI**
scenic	*panor-rar-meeka*	**PANORAMICA**
easy	*fat-cheelay*	**FACILE**
safe	*see-koo-ro*	**SICURO**
Barn	*bar-rac-ka*	**BARACCA**
Bridge	*pon-tay*	**PONTE**
Building	*edee-fee-cheeyo*	**EDIFICIO**
Canal	*ka-nar-lay*	**CANALE**
Church	*kee-ay-za*	**CHIESA**
Cliff	*sko-lee-yair-ra*	**SCOGLIERA**
Crossroads	*een-craw-cho*	**INCROCIO**
Farm	*fattor-ree-ya*	**FATTORIA**
Ferry	*tra-get-toh*	**TRAGHETTO**
Field	*cam-po*	**CAMPO**
Forest	*for-ress-ta*	**FORESTA**

Gate	*can-chay-lo*	**CANCELLO**
Hill	*col-lee-na*	**COLLINA**
House	*cass-sa*	**CASA**
Inn	*loc-kan-da*	**LOCANDA**
Lake	*lar-go*	**LAGO**
Mountain	*mon-tar-nya*	**MONTAGNA**
Path	*vee-yot-toh-lo*	**VIOTTOLO**
Peak	*pee-ko*	**PICCO**
Railway	*fairo-vee-ya*	**FERROVIA**
River	*fee-yoo-mee*	**FIUME**
Road	*strar-da*	**STRADA**
Sea	*mar-ray*	**MARE**
Spring	*sor-jen-tay*	**SORGENTE**
Stream	*tor-ren-tay*	**TORRENTE**
Swamp	*akwee-tree-no*	**ACQUITRINO**
Tree	*al-bairo*	**ALBERO**
Valley	*var-lay*	**VALLE**
Village	*vee-lar-jo*	**VILLAGGIO**
Waterfall	*cass-car-ta*	**CASCATA**

VIETATO L'INGRESSO = NO TRESSPASSING

at	for	from	in	on	to
al	*pair*	*dah*	*een*	*soo*	*ah*
AL	**PER**	**DA**	**IN**	**SU**	**A**

directions: 1   camping: 15   weather: 18B   sports & beach: 20

?

I	*ee-yo* **IO**	would like	*vor-ray-ee* **VORREI**	can I	*poss-o* **POSSO**
we	*noy* **NOI**	would like	*vor-ray-mo* **VORREMMO**	can I have	*poss-o ah-vair-ray* **POSSO AVERE**
you	*lay-ee* **LEI**	want	*vwar-lay* **VUOLE**	Depart	*par-teer-ray* **PARTIRE**
not	*non* **NON**	have	*oh* **HO**	Go	*an-dar-ray* **ANDARE**
no	*non* **NON**	have	*abbee-yar-mo* **ABBIAMO**	Pay	*pa-gar-ray* **PAGARE**
		have	*ah* **HA**	See	*ved-dair-ray* **VEDERE**
				Stay	*ress-tar-ray* **RESTARE**
which	*kwar-lay* **QUALE**	is	*eh* **È**	Take photos	*far-ray fotogra-fee-ya* **FARE FOTOGRAFIA**
where	*doh-vay* **DOVE**	are	*so-no* **SONO**	Reserve	*preno-tar-ray* **PRENOTARE**
what	*koh-sa* **COSA**			Visit	*veezee-tar-ray* **VISITARE**
when	*kwan-doh* **QUANDO**	is there	*chay* **C'È**		

what time	*kay or-ra* **CHE ORA**	entrance	*ayn-trar-ta* **ENTRATA**	reduction	*reedootsee-yo-nay* **RIDUZIONE**
		ticket	*beel-yet-toh* **BIGLIETTO**	group	*groo-po* **GRUPPO**
how long	*kwan-toh tem-po* **QUANTO TEMPO**	per	*al* **AL**	student	*stoo-den-tay* **STUDENTE**
how many	*kwan-tee* **QUANTI**	person	*pair-so-na* **PERSONA**	child/age	*bam-bee-no*/*et-ta* **BAMBINO ETÀ**
how often	*kwan-tay vol-tay* **QUANTE VOLTE**	hour	*or-ra* **ORA**	snr citizen	*cheeta-dee-nee antsee-yar-nee* **CITTADINI ANZIANI**
		day	*jor-no* **GIORNO**		
near	*vee-chee-no* **VICINO**	includes	*com-pray-so* **COMPRESO**	meals	*pas-tee* **PASTI**
here	*kwee* **QUI**				
there	*lar* **LÀ**			HOW MUCH IS THAT?	*kwan-toh coss-ta* **QUANTO COSTA?**
this	*kwess-toh* **QUESTO**				
these	*kwess-tee* **QUESTI**				

	at	by	for	from	in	of	to
	al **AL**	*een* **IN**	*pair* **PER**	*dah* **DA**	*dee* **DI**	*dee* **DI**	*ah* **A**

directions: 1   sightseeing places: 18A   weather: 18B

now	*a-**dess**-o* **ADESSO**		boat	*moto-**scar**-fo* **MOTOSCAFO**
earlier	*pee-**yoo** press-toh* **PIÙ PRESTO**		bus	*owtoh-boos* **AUTOBUS**
later	*pee-**yoo** tar-dee* **PIÙ TARDI**		walking	*passay-**jar**-ray* **PASSEGGIARE**
			trip/tour	*jee-ta* **GITA**
cheaper	***may**-no car-ro* **MENO CARO**		architectural	*arkee-**tet**-too-rarlay* **ARCHITETTURALE**
better	*meel-**yor**-ray* **MIGLIORE**		cultural	*cooltoo-**rar**-lay* **CULTURALE**
air conditioned	*ar-reeya condeetseeo-**nar**-ta* **ARIA CONDIZIONATA**		historical	*stor-reeko* **STORICO**
start	*ee-**neet**-seeyo* **INIZIO**		sceninc	*panor-**rar**-meeka* **PANORAMICA**
finish	*fee-nay* **FINE**		scientific	*shee-en-tee-feeko* **SCIENTIFICO**
open	*a-**pair**-toh* **APERTO**		top	*een **al**-toh* **IN ALTO**
closed	*kee-**oo**-zo* **CHIUSO**		view	*panor-**rar**-ma* **PANORAMA**
guide	*gwee-da* **GUIDA**		son et lumiere	*son ay loomeeyair* **SON ET LUMIÈRE**
guide book	*gwee-da* **GUIDA**		illuminations	*eeloomee-natsee-**yo**-nay* **ILLUMINAZIONI**
map	*mar-pa* **MAPPA**		place	*lwo-go* **LUOGO**
catalogue	*cat-**tar**-lo-go* **CATALOGO**		event	*ay-**ven**-toh* **EVENTO**
English	*eeng-**glay**-zay* **INGLESE**		festival	*fay-sta* **FESTA**
tourist office	*oo-fee-cho too-reess-teeko* **UFFICIO TURISTICO**		today	*od-jee* **OGGI**
ticket office	*beelyetair-ree-ya* **BIGLIETTERIA**		tomorrow	*dom-mar-nee* **DOMANI**
toilets	*toy-let-tay* **TOILETTE**		morning	*mat-tee-no* **MATTINO**
			afternoon	*pommair-**reed**-jo* **POMERIGGIO**
			evening	*sair-ra* **SERA**

ENTRATA LIBERA = ADMISSION FREE
VIETATO FOTOGRAFARE = NO PHOTOGRAPHY

entertainments: 19   **money & tipping: 50A**   **time: 60**

Aquarium	ak-*wair*-reeyo **ACQUARIO**	Gardens	jar-*dee*-nee **GIARDINI**
Ampitheatre	anfee-tay-*yar*-tro **ANFITEATRO**	Harbour	*por*-toh **PORTO**
Art gallery	galair-*ree*-ya *dar*-tay **GALLERIA D'ARTE**	House	*cass*-sa **CASA**
Artist's quarter	kwartee-*yair*-ray *del*-ee ar-*tees*-tee **QUARTIERE DEGLI ARTISTI**	Library	beebleeyo-*tec*-ka **BIBLIOTECA**
		Market	mair-*car*-toh **MERCATO**
Botanical gardens	jar-*dee*-nee bot-*tan*-eechee **GIARDINI BOTANICI**	Monastery	monas-*tair*-ro **MONASTERO**
Building	edee-*fee*-cho **EDIFICIO**	Monument	monoo-*men*-toh **MONUMENTO**
Business district	kwartee-*yair*-ray *del*-ee af-*far*-ree **QUARTIERE DEGLI AFFARI**	Museum	moo-*zay*-yo **MUSEO**
		Old city	chee-*ta vec*-keeya **CITTÀ VECCHIA**
Castle	cass-*tel*-lo **CASTELLO**	Opera house	tay-*yar*-tro del-*lop*-aira **TEATRO DELL'OPERA**
Catacombs	catta-*com*-bay **CATACOMBE**	Palace	pal-*lat*-so **PALAZZO**
Cathedral	catted-*rar*-lay **CATTEDRALE**	Park	*par*-co **PARCO**
Caves	ka-*vair*-nay **CAVERNE**	Ruins	ro-*vee*-nay **ROVINE**
Cemetery	cheemee-*tair*-ro **CIMITERO**	School	*skoo*-oh-la **SCUOLA**
City centre	*chayn*-tro chee-*ta* **CENTRO CITTÀ**	Site	loo-*woh*-go **LUOGO**
Church	kee-*yay*-za **CHIESA**	Stadium	*star*-deeyo **STADIO**
Coliseum	coloss-*say*-yo **COLOSSEO**	Statue	*stat*-toowa **STATUA**
Concert hall	*sar*-la con-*chair*-tee **SALA CONCERTI**	Synagogue	seena-*gog*-ah **SINAGOGA**
Convent	con-*ven*-toh **CONVENTO**	Temple	*tem*-peeyo **TEMPIO**
Downtown area	*chayn*-tro chee-*ta* **CENTRO CITTÀ**	Tower	*tor*-ray **TORRE**
Factory	fab-*ree*-ka **FABBRICA**	University	ooneevairsee-*ta* **UNIVERSITÀ**
Fountain	fon-*tar*-na **FONTANA**	Vinyard	veen-*yet*-toh **VIGNETO**
Fort	for-*tet*-sa **FORTEZZA**	Zoo	*tsoo*-oh **ZOO**

subjects: 22B   industries: 23   arts & antiques: 41B   jewelry: 42B

?

not	*non* **NON**	
no	*non* **NON**	
what	*koh-sa* **COSA**	
when	*kwan-doh* **QUANDO**	

how long *kwan-toh tem-po* **QUANTO TEMPO**

this *kwess-toh* **QUESTO**

do you know	*sa* **SA**
if	*say* **SE**
will it be	*sa-rah* **SARÀ**
is	*eh* **È**
it is	*eh* **È**

Continue	*prossay-gwee-ray* **PROSEGUIRE**
Improve	*meeleeyor-rar-ray* **MIGLIORARE**
Rain	*peeyo-vairay* **PIOVERE**
Snow	*nayvee-kar-ray* **NEVICARE**
Worsen	*payjo-rar-ray* **PEGGIORARE**

maybe	*for-say* **FORSE**
good	*bwoh-no* **BUONO**
bad	*cat-tee-vo* **CATTIVO**
lovely	*bel-la* **BELLA**
much	*mol-toh* **MOLTO**
more	*pee-yoo* **PIÙ**
less	*may-no* **MENO**
very	*mol-toh* **MOLTO**

Changeable *varree-yar-beelay* **VARIABILE**

Cloudy	*noovol-lo-so* **NUVOLOSO**
Dry	*sec-ko* **SECCO**
Foggy	*neb-beeya* **NEBBIA**
Hazy	*broo-mo-so* **BRUMOSO**
Humid	*oo-meedoh* **UMIDO**
Icy	*jel-leedoh* **GELIDO**
Rain	*pee-yod-ja* **PIOGGIA**
Rainy	*peeyo-vo-so* **PIOVOSO**
Snow	*nay-vay* **NEVE**
Snowy	*nay-vo-so* **NEVOSO**
Stormy	*tempess-toh-so* **TEMPESTOSO**
Sunny	*solair-jee-yartoh* **SOLEGGIATO**
Windy	*ven-toh-so* **VENTOSO**

forecast for: *preveezee-yo-nay pair:* **PREVISIONI PER:**

today	*od-jee* **OGGI**
tomorrow	*dom-mar-nee* **DOMANI**
morning	*mat-tee-no* **MATTINO**
afternoon	*pommair-reed-jo* **POMERIGGIO**
evening	*sair-ra* **SERA**

Temperature *tempaira-too-ra* **TEMPERATURA**

hot	*cal-doh* **CALDO**
warm	*cal-doh* **CALDO**
mild	*mee-tay* **MITE**
cool	*fres-co* **FRESCO**
cold	*fray-doh* **FREDDO**
freezing	*jel-lo* **GELO**

north
nord
NORD

west *oh-vest* **OVEST**		east *est* **EST**

south
sood
SUD

?	I	*ee-yo* **IO**
	we	*noy* **NOI**
	you	*lay-ee* **LEI**
	who	*kee* **CHI**
	not	*non* **NON**
	no	*non* **NON**
	which	*kwar-lay* **QUALE**
	where	*doh-vay* **DOVE**
	when	*kwan-doh* **QUANDO**
	what	*koh-sa* **COSA**
	what time	*kay or-ra* **CHE ORA**
	what's on	*koh-sa chay* **COSA C'È**
	how long	*kwan-toh tem-po* **QUANTO TEMPO**
	how many	*kwan-tee* **QUANTI**
	near	*vee-chee-no* **VICINO**
	here	*kwee* **QUI**
	there	*lar* **LÀ**
	this	*kwess-toh* **QUESTO**

would like	*vor-ray-ee* **VORREI**	is there	*chay* **C'È**
would like	*vor-ray-mo* **VORREMMO**	can I	*poss-o* **POSSO**
want	*vwar-lay* **VUOLE**	can I have	*poss-o ah-vair-ray* **POSSO AVERE**
have	*oh* **HO**	Dance	*bal-lar-ray* **BALLARE**
have	*abbee-yar-mo* **ABBIAMO**	Go	*an-dar-ray* **ANDARE**
have	*ah* **HA**	Like	*peeya-chair-ray* **PIACERE**
do you have	*ah-vet-tay* **AVETE**	Reserve	*preno-tar-ray* **PRENOTARE**
is	*eh* **È**	Pay	*pa-gar-ray* **PAGARE**
are	*so-no* **SONO**	See	*ved-dair-ray* **VEDERE**

ticket	*beel-yet-toh* **BIGLIETTO**	table	*tar-vo-lo* **TAVOLO**
reduction	*reedootsee-yo-nay* **RIDUZIONE**	seat	*poss-toh* **POSTO**
group	*groo-po* **GRUPPO**	balcony	*gallair-ree-ya* **GALLERIA**
student	*stoo-den-tay* **STUDENTE**	stalls	*plat-tay-ya* **PLATEA**
child/age	*bam-bee-no*/*et-ta* **BAMBINO ETÀ**	front	*fron-tay* **FRONTE**
snr citizen	*cheeta-dee-nee antsee-yar-nee* **CITTADINI ANZIANI**	middle	*met-so* **MEZZO**
identity	*eedentee-ta* **IDENTITÀ**	back	*postairee-yor-ray* **POSTERIORE**

HOW MUCH IS (THAT)? *kwan-toh coss-ta* **QUANTO COSTA?**

at	by	for	from	in	of	to
al **AL**	*dee* **DI**	*pair* **PER**	*dah* **DA**	*een* **IN**	*dee* **DI**	*ah* **A**

money & tipping: 50A   time: 60

cheaper	*may-no **car**-ro* **MENO CARO**		Ballet	*bal-**let**-toh* **BALLETTO**
better	*meel-**yor**-ray* **MIGLIORE**		Concert	*con-**chair**-toh* **CONCERTO**
alternative	*altairna-**tee**-va* **ALTERNATIVA**		Film/Movie	*feelm* **FILM**
			(subtitles/dubbed)	(*sot-toh **tee**-tolee/doppee-**yar**-toh*) **(SOTTO TITOLI DOPPIATO)**
now	*a-**dess**-o* **ADESSO**		(English)	(*eeng-**glay**-zay*) **(INGLESE)**
later	*pee-**yoo** tar-dee* **PIÙ TARDI**		Musical	*oppair-**ret**-ta* **OPERETTA**
starts	*ee-**neet**-seeyo* **INIZIO**		Opera	*op-**paira*** **OPERA**
finishes	*fee-nay* **FINE**		Play	*pro-sah* **PROSA**
today	*od-jee* **OGGI**		Revue	*ree-**veess**-ta* **RIVISTA**
tomorrow	*dom-**mar**-nee* **DOMANI**		programme	*pro-**grar**-ma* **PROGRAMMA**
matinee	*matee-**nay*** **MATINÈE**			
evening	*sair-ra* **SERA**		Cinema	*chee-nayma* **CINEMA**
			Concert hall	*sar-la con-**chair**-tee* **SALA CONCERTI**
singing	*can-ta* **CANTA**		Opera house	*tay-**yar**-tro del-**lop**-paira* **TEATRO DELL'OPERA**
dancing	*bar-la* **BALLA**		Theatre	*tay-**yar**-tro* **TEATRO**
performance	*spet-**tac**-ko-lo* **SPETTACOLO**			
classical	*clas-seeko* **CLASSICO**		entrance fee	*pret-so dayn-**trar**-ta* **PREZZO D'ENTRATA**
modern	*mod-**dair**-no* **MODERNO**		Cabaret	*cab-bar-ray* **CABARET**
traditional	*tradeetseeyo-**nar**-lay* **TRADIZIONALE**		Dance hall	*sar-la dah **bar**-lo* **SALA DA BALLO**
casual dress	*casual* **CASUAL**		Discotheque	*deesco-**tecka*** **DISCOTECA**
evening dress	*ar-**beetoh** dah **sair**-ra* **ABITO DA SERA**		Folk club	*folk cloob* **FOLK CLUB**
cloakroom	*gwar-da-**ro**-ba* **GUARDAROBA**		Jazz club	*jazz cloob* **JAZZ CLUB**
toilet	*toy-**let**-tay* **TOILETTE**		Night club	*night cloob* **NIGHT CLUB**

more types of music: 44B

?

I	*ee-yo* **IO**	would like	*vor-**ray**-ee* **VORREI**	is	*eh* **È**
me	*may* **ME**	would like	*vor-**ray**-mo* **VORREMMO**	are	*so-no* **SONO**
we	*noy* **NOI**	want	*vwar-lay* **VUOLE**	is there	*chay* **C'È**
us	*noy* **NOI**	have	*oh* **HO**		
you	*lay-ee* **LEI**	have	*abbee-**yar**-mo* **ABBIAMO**	Go	*an-**dar**-ray* **ANDARE**
		have	*ah* **HA**	Buy	*com-**prar**-ray* **COMPRARE**
not	*non* **NON**	can I	*poss-o* **POSSO**	Like	*peeya-**chair**-ray* **PIACERE**
no	*non* **NON**	can I have	*poss-o ah-**vair**-ray* **POSSO AVERE**	Play	*joc-**kar**-ray* **GIOCARE**
where	*doh-vay* **DOVE**	can we	*possee-**yar**-mo* **POSSIAMO**	Rent	*noled-**jar**-ray* **NOLEGGIARE**
when	*kwan-doh* **QUANDO**	can you	*pwoh* **PUÒ**	Take part	*partaychee-**par**-ray* **PARTECIPARE**
what	*koh-sa* **COSA**			Watch	*gwar-**dar**-ray* **GUARDARE**

		ticket	*beel-**yet**-toh* **BIGLIETTO**	reduction	*reedootsee-**yo**-nay* **RIDUZIONE**
what time	*kay **or**-ra* **CHE ORA**	the charge	*eel **pret**-so* **IL PREZZO**	student	*stoo-**den**-tay* **STUDENTE**
what's on	*koh-sa chay* **COSA C'È**	per	*ah* **A**	child	*bam-**bee**-no* **BAMBINO**
		person	*pair-**so**-na* **PERSONA**	age	*et-**ta*** **ETÀ**
how long	*kwan-toh **tem**-po* **QUANTO TEMPO**	session	*sessee-**yo**-nay* **SESSIONE**	lesson	*letsee-**yo**-nee* **LEZIONI**
how many	*kwan-tee* **QUANTI**	hour	*or-ra* **ORA**	permit	*pair-**mess**-o* **PERMESSO**
		day	*jor-no* **GIORNO**	equipment	*ekweeparja-**men**-toh* **EQUIPAGGIAMENTO**

near	*vee-**chee**-no* **VICINO**
here	*kwee* **QUI**
there	*lar* **LÀ**
this	*kwess-toh* **QUESTO**

HOW MUCH IS (THAT)? *kwan-toh **coss**-ta* **QUANTO COSTA?**

at	for	from	in	on	to	with
al **AL**	*pair* **PER**	*dah* **DA**	*een* **IN**	*soo* **SU**	*ah* **A**	*con* **CON**

types of sports: 21A   weather: 18B   money & tipping: 50A   time: 60

conditions	*condeetsee-**yo**-nee* **CONDIZIONI**		Course	***cam***-po **CAMPO**
very	***mol***-toh **MOLTO**		Courts	***cam***-pee **CAMPI**
good	***bwoh***-no **BUONO**		Gymnasium	*pal-**less**-tra* **PALESTRA**
bad	*cat-**tee**-vo* **CATTIVO**		Lake	***lar***-go **LAGO**
busy	*affol-**lar**-toh* **AFFOLLATO**		Race track	***peess***-ta **PISTA**
quiet	*trang-**kwee**-lo* **TRANQUILLO**		River	*fee-**yoo**-may* **FIUME**
dangerous	*paireecol-**lo**-so* **PERICOLOSO**		Sports centre	***cass***-sa dello sport **CASA DELLO SPORT**
safe	*see-**koo**-ro* **SICURO**		Sports ground	***cam***-po dello sport **CAMPO DELLO SPORT**
somewhere	*dah **kwal**-kay **par**-tay* **DA QUALCHE PARTE**		Swimming pool	*pee-**shee**-na* **PISCINA**
near	*vee-**chee**-no* **VICINO**			
nearest	*pee-**yoo** vee-**chee**-no* **PIÙ VICINO**		BEACH	*spee-**yad**-ja* **SPIAGGIA**
open	*a-**pair**-toh* **APERTO**		private	*pree-**var**-ta* **PRIVATA**
closed	*kee-**oo**-zo* **CHIUSO**		Air mattress	*lie-lo* **LILO**
start	*ee-**neet**-seeyo* **INIZIO**		Boat	***bar***-ka **BARCA**
finish	***fee***-nay **FINE**		Children	*bam-**bee**-nee* **BAMBINI**
beginner	*preenchee-**pee**-yantay* **PRINCIPIANTE**		Currents	*cor-**ren**-tee* **CORRENTI**
average	***med***-eeya **MEDIA**		Jelly fish	*med-**doo**-zay* **MEDUSE**
experienced	*ays-**pair**-toh* **ESPERTO**		Lifeguard	*ban-**yee**-no* **BAGNINO**
professional	*professeeyo-**nar**-lay* **PROFESSIONALE**		Sea	***mar***-ray **MARE**
player	*jocka-**tor**-ray* **GIOCATORE**		Sunshade	*ombrel-**lo**-nay* **OMBRELLONE**
team	***skward***-ra **SQUADRA**		Surf board	***tar***-vo-la dah soorf **TAVOLA DA SURF**
			Tide	*mar-**ray**-ya* **MAREA**
			(high/low)	*(alta/bassa)* **(ALTA BASSA)**

---

equipment: 21B   **family needs: 26**

tournament	*tor-**nay**-yo* **TORNEO**		Gliding	*al-**lee**-yantay* **ALIANTE**
race	*cor-sa* **CORSA**		Golf	*golf* **GOLF**
game	*par-**tee**-ta* **PARTITA**		Gymnastics	*at-**let**-teeka led-**jair**-ra* **ATLETICA LEGGERA**
match	*par-**tee**-ta* **PARTITA**		Hang gliding	*delta-**play**-no* **DELTAPLANO**
			Hiking	*cammee-**nar**-ray* **CAMMINARE**
Archery	*tee-ro col-**lar**-co* **TIRO COLL'ARCO**		Hockey	*hock-ayee* **HOCKEY**
Athletics	*at-**let**-teeka* **ATLETICA**		Horse racing	*cor-sa dee ka-**val**-lee* **CORSA DI CAVALLI**
Badminton	*vol-**lar**-no* **VOLANO**		Horse riding	*caval-**car**-ray* **CAVALCARE**
Baseball	*baseball* **BASEBALL**		Hunting	*car-**chee**-ya ah ka-**val**-lo* **CACCIA A CAVALLO**
Basket ball	*palla-can-**nay**-stro* **PALLACANESTRO**		Ice skating	*pattee-**nar**-jo sool ghee-**atch**-o* **PATTINAGGIO SUL GHIACCIO**
Billiards	*beelee-**yar**-doh* **BILIARDO**		Judo	*judo* **JUDO**
BMX	*chee-klee bee emmay eex* **CICLI BMX**		Keep fit	*jee-**nass**-teeka* **GINNASTICA**
Bowling	*bot-chay* **BOCCE**		Lacrosse	*lacross* **LACROSSE**
Boxing	*poojee-**lar**-toh* **PUGILATO**		Martial arts	*ar-tee martsee-**yar**-lee* **ARTI MARZIALI**
Canoeing	*canno-**tar**-jo* **CANOTTAGGIO**		Motor racing	*cor-sa dee **mak**-keena* **CORSA DI MACCHINA**
Climbing	*skal-**lar**-ray* **SCALARE**		Motorcycle racing	*cor-sa dee motochee-**klet**-tay* **CORSA DI MOTOCICLETTE**
Cricket	*cricket* **CRICKET**		Motocross	*motocross* **MOTOCROSS**
Cycling	*chee-**kleess**-mo* **CICLISMO**		Net ball	*pal-la ah **ray**-tay* **PALLA A RETE**
Fencing	*skair-ma* **SCHERMA**		Parachuting	*parrakadoo-**teess**-mo* **PARACADUTISMO**
Fishing	*pess-**car**-ray* **PESCARE**		Polo	*polo* **POLO**
Football (EU)	*cal-cheeo* **CALCIO**		Pot holing	*spaylay-ollo-**jee**-ya* **SPELEOLOGIA**
Football (US)	*cal-cheeo amairee-**car**-no* **CALCIO AMERICANO**		Rowing	*canno-**tad**-jo* **CANOTTAGGIO**
Flying	*vol-oh* **VOLO**		Roller skating	*pattee-**nad**-jo ah rot-**tel**-lay* **PATTINAGGIO A ROTELLE**

other recreations: 22B

English	Pronunciation	Italian
Rugby	*roog-by*	**RUGBY**
Running	*cor-rair-ray*	**CORRERE**
Sailing	*vel-ed-jar-ray*	**VELEGGIARE**
Scuba diving	*scoo-ba*	**SCUBA**
Ski-ing	*shee-yar-ray*	**SCIARE**
Skin diving	*too-far-see een ap-naya*	**TUFFARSI IN APNEA**
Shooting	*car-cheeya*	**CACCIA**
Snooker	*car-ram-bo-la*	**CARAMBOLA**
Snorkelling	*far-ray lo snorkel*	**FARE LO SNORKEL**
Soccer	*cal-cheeo*	**CALCIO**
Softball	*softball*	**SOFTBALL**
Speedboat racing	*gar-ra dee moto-scar-fee*	**GARA DI MOTOSCAFI**
Squash	*squash*	**SQUASH**
Surfing	*akwa-play-no*	**ACQUAPLANO**
Swimming pool	*noowo-tar-ray*	**NUOTARE**
Table tennis	*ping pong*	**PING PONG**
Tennis	*tennis*	**TENNIS**
Tobogganing	*sport del toh-bog-gan*	**SPORT DEL TOBOGGAN**
Volley ball	*pal-la vol-lo*	**PALLA VOLO**
Walking	*pass-ed-jar-ray*	**PASSEGGIARE**
Water polo	*po-lo dak-wa*	**POLO D'ACQUA**
Water ski-ing	*shee a-kwat-eeko*	**SCI ACQUATICO**
Wrestling	*lotta lee-bair-ra*	**LOTTA LIBERA**

EQUIPMENT	*ekwee-parja-men-toh*	**EQUIPAGGIAMENTO**
ball	*pal-la*	**PALLA**
bat	*mat-sa*	**MAZZA**
boat	*barc-ka*	**BARCA**
boots	*stee-var-lee*	**STIVALI**
bowls	*bot-chay*	**BOCCE**
fishing rod	*kan-nah dah pes-ka*	**CANNA DA PESCA**
golf clubs	*mat-say dah golf*	**MAZZE DA GOLF**

canoe	*ka-no-wah*	**CANOA**
ski poles	*bass-toh-nee*	**BASTONI**
racquet	*rac-ket-ta*	**RACCHETTA**
skates	*pat-teenee*	**PATTINI**
skis	*shee*	**SCI**
ski boots	*scar-po-nee*	**SCARPONI**
ski lift	*shee lift*	**SCI LIFT**

CHESS	*skar-kee*	**SCACCHI**
king	*ray*	**RE**
queen	*ray-jee-na*	**REGINA**
castle	*tor-ray*	**TORRE**
bishop	*alfee-yair-ray*	**ALFIERE**
knight	*ka-val-lo*	**CAVALLO**
pawn	*ped-dee-na*	**PEDINA**

CHECK	*skar-ko*	**SCACCO**
MATE	*mar-toh*	**MATTO**

CARDS	*car-tay*	**CARTE**
jack	*fan-tay*	**FANTÉ**
joker	*mat-ta*	**MATTA**
hearts	*kwor-ree*	**CUORI**
diamonds	*kward-ree*	**QUADRI**
clubs	*fee-yor-ree*	**FIORI**
spades	*pee-kay*	**PICCHE**

I'M OUT!	*mee ree-tee-ro*	**MI RITIRO**

Bridge	**BRIDGE**
Canasta	**CANASTA**
Gin Rummy	**RAMINO**
Whist	**WHIST**
Pontoon/21	**TRESETTE**
Poker	**POKER**

?

I	*ee-yo* **IO**	would like	*vor-ray-ee* **VORREI**
me	*may* **ME**	would like	*vor-ray-mo* **VORREMMO**
we	*noy* **NOI**	want	*vwar-lay* **VUOLE**
us	*noy* **NOI**	have	*oh* **HO**
you	*lay-ee* **LEI**	have	*abbee-yar-mo* **ABBIAMO**
		have	*ah* **HA**
not	*non* **NON**	am	*so-no* **SONO**
no	*non* **NON**	is	*eh* **È**
		are	*so-no* **SONO**
which	*kwar-lay* **QUALE**		
where	*doh-vay* **DOVE**	is there	*chay* **C'È**
when	*kwan-doh* **QUANDO**		
what	*koh-sa* **COSA**		

can I	*poss-o* **POSSO**
can I have	*poss-o ah-vair-ray* **POSSO AVERE**
can we	*posse-yar-mo* **POSSIAMO**
can you	*pwoh* **PUÒ**
Buy	*com-prar-ray* **COMPRARE**
Do	*far-ray* **FARE**
Interested in	*appaseeyo-nar-toh dee* **APPASSIONATO DI**
Like	*peeya-chair-ray* **PIACERE**
Meet	*eencon-trar-ray* **INCONTRARE**
Play	*joc-kar-ray* **GIOCARE**
Rent	*affee-tar-ray* **AFFITTARE**

		club	*cheer-ko-lo* **CIRCOLO**	somewhere	*dah kwal-kay par-tay* **DA QUALCHE PARTE**
what time	*kay or-ra* **CHE ORA**	people	*jen-tay* **GENTE**	anyone	*oh-yoo-no* **AGNUNO**
		place	*loo-woh-go* **LUOGO**	open	*a-pair-toh* **APERTO**
how long	*kwan-toh tem-po* **QUANTO TEMPO**	shop	*neg-go-seeyo* **NEGOZIO**	closed	*kee-oo-zo* **CHIUSO**
how many	*kwan-tee* **QUANTI**	game	*par-tee-ta* **PARTITA**	beginner	*preenchee-pee-yantay* **PRINCIPIANTE**
how often	*kwan-tay vol-tay* **QUANTE VOLTE**	equipment	*ekwee-parja-men-toh* **EQUIPAGGIAMENTO**	average	*med-eeya* **MEDIA**
		instruction	*eestrootstee-yo-nay* **ISTRUZIONE**	experienced	*ays-pair-toh* **ESPERTO**
near	*vee-chee-no* **VICINO**				
here	*kwee* **QUI**				
there	*lar* **LÀ**				

	at	for	from	in	on	to	with
	al **AL**	*pair* **PER**	*dah* **DA**	*dee* **DI**	*soo* **SU**	*ah* **A**	*con* **CON**

---

money: 50A   **time & meeting: 60**

Amateur dramatics	**FILODRAMMATICA**	History	**STORIA**
Antiques	**ANTICHITÀ**	Insects	**INSETTI**
Architecture	**ARCHITETTURA**	Knitting	**LAVORI A MAGLIA**
Art	**ARTE**	Languages	**LINGUE**
Astronomy	**ASTRONOMIA**	Marine biology	**BIOLOGIA MARINA**
Backgammon	**TRIC-TRAC**	Mathematics	**MATEMATICA**
Ballet	**BALLETTO**	Mechanics	**MECCANICA**
Bird watching	**ORNITOLOGIA**	Metalwork	**LAVORI IN METALLO**
Boating	**CANOTTAGGIO**	Models	**MODELLI**
Botany	**BOTANICA**	(airplanes)	**(AREOPLANI)**
Calligraphy	**CALLIGRAFIA**	(boats)	**(NAVI/BARCHE)**
Camping	**CAMPEGGIO**	(buses/trams)	**(BUS/TRAM)**
Cards (playing)	**CARTE DA GIOCO**	(railways)	**(FERROVIE)**
Carpentry	**FALEGNAMERIA**	Motorcycling	**MOTOCICLISMO**
Cars	**AUTOMOBILI**	Music	**MUSICA**
Chemistry	**CHIMICA**	(classical/jazz)	**(CLASSICA/JAZZ)**
Chess	**SCACCHI**	(folk/pop)	**(FOLK/POP)**
Cinema	**CINEMA**	Natural history	**STORIA NATURALE**
Collecting	**COLLEZIONARE**	Needlework	**RICAMO**
Concerts	**CONCERTI**	Opera	**OPERA**
Conservation	**CONSERVAZIONE**	Painting	**PITTURA**
Computers	**COMPUTERS**	Pets	**ANIMALI DOMESTICI**
Cooking	**CULINARIA**	Photography	**FOTOGRAFIA**
Crafts	**ARTIGIANATO**	Physics	**FISICA**
Current affairs	**ATTUALITÀ**	Politics	**POLITICA**
Cycling	**CICLISMO**	(communist)	**(COMUNISTA)**
Dancing	**DANZA**	(social democrat)	**(SOCIALISTI DEM.)**
(ballroom)	**(SALA DA BALLO)**	(centre/right)	**(CENTRO/DESTRA)**
(folk/pop)	**(FOLK/POP)**	(far right)	**(ESTREMA DESTRA)**
Darts	**FRECCETTE**	Pottery	**CERAMICA**
Debating	**DIBATTITI**	Reading	**LETTURA**
Design	**DISEGNO**	Science	**SCIENZA**
Draughts	**DAMA**	Sculpture	**SCULTURA**
Drawing	**DISEGNO**	Singing	**CANTO**
Electronics	**ELETTRONICA**	Social sciences	**SCIENZE SOCIALI**
Environment	**AMBIENTE**	Space	**SPAZIO**
Fashion	**MODE**	Sports	**SPORT**
Fish	**PESCE**	Stamp collecting	**FILATELIA**
Fishing	**PESCA**	Theatre	**TEATRO**
Flower arranging	**COMPOSIZIONE CON FIORI**	Transport	**TRASPORTO**
Gardening	**GIARDINAGGIO**	(see models)	(vedi modelli)
Gardens	**GIARDINI**	Travelling	**VIAGGIARE**
Geography	**GEOGRAFIA**	Tv/radio	**TV & RADIO**
Geology	**GEOLOGIA**	Walking	**PASSEGGIARE**
Handicrafts	**ARTIGIANATO**	Weaving	**TESSERE**
Hiking	**ESCURSIONI A PIEDI**	Writing	**SCRIVERE**

sports: 21   chess & cards: 21B   arts & antiques: 41   types of music: 44B

?

I	*ee-yo* **IO**	would like	*vor-ray-ee* **VORREI**
my	*eel mee-yo* **IL MIO**	would like	*vor-ray-mo* **VORREMMO**
we	*noy* **NOI**	want	*vwar-lay* **VUOLE**
you	*lay-ee* **LEI**		
		have	*oh* **HO**
		have	*ah* **HA**
not	*non* **NON**		
no	*non* **NON**	am	*so-no* **SONO**
		is	*eh* **È**
		are	*so-no* **SONO**

Change	*cambee-yar-ray* **CAMBIARE**
Do	*far-ray* **FARE**
Like	*peeya-chair-ray* **PIACERE**
See	*ved-dair-ray* **VEDERE**
Show me	*mee moss-tree* **MI MOSTRI**
Studying	*stoo-deeyo* **STUDIO**
Training	*apprendee-star-toh* **APPRENDISTATO**
Visit	*veezee-tar-ray* **VISITARE**
Work	*lavor-rar-ray* **LAVORARE**

which	*kwar-lay* **QUALE**	
where	*doh-vay* **DOVE**	
when	*kwan-doh* **QUANDO**	
what	*koh-sa* **COSA**	

	College	*col-led-jo* **COLLEGIO**	government	*go-vair-no* **GOVERNO**
	Clinic	*clee-neeka* **CLINICA**	local govt	*mooneechee-palee-ta* **MUNICIPALITÀ**
	Factory	*fab-reeka* **FABBRICA**	private Co	*compa-nee-ya pree-var-ta* **COMPAGNIA PRIVATA**
how long	*kwan-toh tem-po* **QUANTO TEMPO**	Farm	*fattor-ree-ya* **FATTORIA**	state Co	*compa-nee-ya sta-tar-lay* **COMPAGNIA STATALE**
	Hospital	*osped-dar-lay* **OSPEDALE**	self-emp	*lavora-tor-ray ow-ton-om-mo* **LAVORATORE AUTONOMO**
near	*vee-chee-no* **VICINO**	Laboratory	*labora-tor-reeyo* **LABORATORIO**	large	*gran-day* **GRANDE**
here	*kwee* **QUI**	Office	*oo-fee-cho* **UFFICIO**	small	*pee-ko-lo* **PICCOLO**
there	*lar* **LÀ**	School	*skwoh-la* **SCUOLA**		
		Shop	*neg-go-tseeyo* **NEGOZIO**	name	*no-may* **NOME**
		Warehouse	*magga-zee-no* **MAGAZZINO**	address	*eendee-reet-so* **INDIRIZZO**
start	*ee-neet-seeyo* **INIZIO**			
finish	*fee-nay* **FINE**			
quit	*la-shar-toh* **LASCIATO**			

at	for	from	in	to	with
al	*pair*	*dah*	*een*	*ah*	*con*
AL	**PER**	**DA**	**IN**	**A**	**CON**

countries & places: 24 & 25   **time & meeting: 60**

JOB	*eem-**pee**-yaygo*	INDUSTRY	*een-**doo**-streeya*
	IMPIEGO		**INDUSTRIA**
housewife	**CASALINGA**	Aerospace	**AEROSPAZIALE**
retired	**PENSIONATO**	Airline	**LINEA AEREA**
unemployed	**DISOCCUPATO**	Banking	**BANCARIA**
worker	**LAVORATORE**	Broadcasting	**RADIODIFFUSIONE**
		Building materials	**EDILIZIA**
Accountant	**CONTABILE**	Bus	**AUTOBUS**
Actor	**ATTORE**	Car	**AUTOMOBILE**
Architect	**ARCHITETTO**	Catering	**FORNITORE DI VITTO**
Artist	**ARTISTA**	Chemical	**CHIMICA**
Administrator	**AMMINISTRATORE**	Clothing	**ABBIGLIAMENTO**
Assembler	**MONTATORE**	Construction	**COSTRUZIONE**
Chef	**CUOCO**	Computer	**COMPUTERS**
Clerk	**IMPIEGATO**	Domestic goods	**CASALINGHI**
Designer	**DISEGNATORE**	Electrical equipment	**ATTREZZATURA ELETTRICA**
Doctor	**DOTTORE**	Electrical supply	**MERCE ELETTRICA**
Driver	**AUTISTA**	Electronics	**ELETTRONICA**
Electrician	**ELETTRICISTA**	Entertainment	**SPETTACOLO**
Engineer	**INGEGNERE**	Farming	**AGRARIA**
Fireman	**POMPIERE**	Food processing	**INDUSTRIE ALIMENTARI**
Inspector	**ISPETTORE**	Forestry	**FORESTALE**
Journalist	**GIORNALISTA**	Furniture	**MOBILI**
Lawyer	**AVVOCATO**	Glass	**INDUSTRIA VETRARIA**
Librarian	**BIBLIOTECARIO**	Health	**SALUTE/IGIENE**
Linguist	**LINGUISTA**	Hotel	**ALBERGHIERA**
Manager	**GERENTE**	Insurance	**ASSICURAZIONE**
Mechanic	**MECCANICO**	Leisure	**TEMPO DI SVAGO**
Musician	**MUSICISTA**	Machinery	**MACCHINARI**
Nurse	**INFERMIERA**	Military	**MILITARE**
Painter	**PITTORE**	Mining	**MINIERA**
Photographer	**FOTOGRAFO**	Newspapers	**STAMPA**
Planner	**PIANIFICATORE**	Oil	**PETROLIO**
Plumber	**IDRAULICO**	Paper	**CARTA**
Policeman	**POLIZIOTTO**	Plastics	**PLASTICA**
Politician	**POLITICO**	Postal	**POSTALE**
Programmer	**PROGRAMMATORE**	Pottery	**CERAMICA**
Salesperson	**COMMESSO/A**	Printing	**TIPOGRAFIA**
Scientist	**SCIENZIATO**	Publishing	**EDITORIALE**
Secretary	**SEGRETARIA/O**	Railways	**FERROVIE**
Socialworker	**ASSISTENTE SOCIALE**	Retail	**VENDITA AL MINUTO**
Student	**STUDENTE**	Road haulage	**TRASPORTO MERCI SU STRADA**
Teacher	**INSEGNANTE**	Steel	**ACCIAIO**
Technician	**TECNICO**	Telecommunications	**COMMUNICAZIONI**
Waiter/ress	**CAMERIERE/A**	Textiles	**TESSILI**
Writer	**SCRITTORE**	Timber	**LEGNAME-LEGNO**

other subjects: 22B

?

I	*ee-yo* **IO**		
my	*eel mee-yo* **IL MIO**		
we	*noy* **NOI**		
our	*noss-tro* **NOSTRO**		
you	*lay-ee* **LEI**		
your	*eel soo-oh* **IL SUO**		
not	*non* **NON**		
no	*non* **NON**		

would like	*vor-ray-ee* **VORREI**	is there	*chay* **C'È**
would like	*vor-ray-mo* **VORREMMO**		
want	*vwar-lay* **VUOLE**	Come from	*ven-nee-ray dah* **VENIRE DA**
		Go	*an-dar-ray* **ANDARE**
have	*oh* **HO**	Like	*peeya-chair-ray* **PIACERE**
have	*abbee-yar-mo* **ABBIAMO**	Live	*arbee-tar-ray* **ABITARE**
have	*ah* **HA**	Stay	*ress-tar-ray* **RESTARE**
is	*eh* **È**	Visit	*veezee-tar-ray* **VISITARE**
are	*so-no* **SONO**	Work	*lavor-rar-ray* **LAVORARE**

where	*doh-vay* **DOVE**	name	*no-may* **NOME**	before	*pree-ma* **PRIMA**
when	*kwan-doh* **QUANDO**	address	*eendee-reet-so* **INDIRIZZO**	now	*a-dess-o* **ADESSO**
what	*koh-sa* **COSA**	large	*gran-day* **GRANDE**	after	*dor-po* **DOPO**
		small	*pee-ko-lo* **PICCOLO**	family	*fa-meel-ya* **FAMIGLIA**
how long	*kwan-toh tem-po* **QUANTO TEMPO**	City	*chee-ta* **CITTÀ**	home	*cass-sa* **CASA**
how far	*kwan-toh dees-tan-tay* **QUANTO DISTANTE**	Coast	*coss-ta* **COSTA**	place	*loo-wo-ghee* **LUOGHI**
		Country	*par-ay-zay* **PAESE**	business	*af-far-ree* **AFFARI**
near	*vee-chee-no* **VICINO**	Countryside	*cam-parn-ya* **CAMPAGNA**	study	*stoo-deeyo* **STUDIO**
here	*kwee* **QUI**	Suburb	*pairreefair-ree-ya* **PERIFERIA**	vacation	*vac-cant-say* **VACANZE**
there	*lar* **LÀ**	Village	*vee-lar-jeeyo* **VILLAGGIO**	tour	*vee-zeeta* **VISITA**

best	*meel-yor-ray* **MIGLIORE**	and	at	for	from	in	of	to	with
other	*al-tro* **ALTRO**	*ay* **E**	*al* **AL**	*pair* **PER**	*dah* **DA**	*een* **IN**	*dee* **DI**	*ah* **A**	*con* **CON**

SWITZERLAND
sweet-sairra
SVIZZERA

lok-kar-no
LOCARNO

AUSTRIA
ows-treeya
AUSTRIA

Turin
*toh-**ree**-no*
TORINO

ko-mo
COMO

bair-gammo
BERGAMO

kor-tee-na
CORTINA

FRANCE
fran-cheeya
FRANCIA

Milan
mee-lar-no
MILANO

*aless-**san**-dreeya*
ALESSANDRIA ●

trayn-toh
TRENTO

man-tohva
MANTOVA

vair-ro-no
VERONA

Venice
*ven-**net**-seeya*
VENEZIA

*oo-**dee**-nay*
UDINE

Genoa
jay-nova
GENOVA

*pa-**vee**-ya*
PAVIA

par-ma
PARMA

pad-ohva
PADOVA

tree-ess-tay
TRIESTE

san ray-mo
SAN REMO

La spayt-seeya
LA SPEZIA

*mo-**dair**-na*
MODENA

*fair-**rar**-ra*
FERRARA

yay-zolo
JESOLO

YUGOSLAVIA
yugo-slar-via
IUGOSLAVIA

*bol-**lon**-ya*
BOLOGNA

*ra-**ven**-na*
RAVENNA

lee-vor-no
LIVORNO

pee-za
PISA

Florence
fee-rent-say
FIRENZE

ree-meenee
RIMINI

pay-zarro
PESARO

CORSICA

see-yen-na
SIENA

san ma-ree-no
SAN MARINO

ah-ret-so
AREZZO

an-ko-na
ANCONA

pair-roo-ja
PERUGIA

*ass-**see**-zee*
ASSISI

tair-nee
TERNI

lak-weela
L'AQUILA

Rome
ro-ma
ROMA

pess-kar-ra
PESCARA

SARDINIA
*sar-**dayn**-ya*
SARDEGNA

*oss-**teeya***
OSTIA

ITALY
*ee-**tal**-ya*
ITALIA

Adriatic Sea
*mar-ray addree-**yat**-eeko*
MARE ADRIATICO

kal-yarree
CAGLIARI

fod-ja
FOGGIA

Naples
nap-polee
NAPOLI

bar-let-ta
BARLETTA

*pom-**pay**-ee*
POMPEII

bah-ree
BARI

Mediterranean Sea
*mar-ray medeetair-**rar**-nayo*
MARE MEDITERRANEO

*sor-**ren**-toh*
SORRENTO

*sal-**lair**-no*
SALERNO

ta-ran-toh
TARANTO

breen-deezee
BRINDISI

*ko-**zent**-sa*
COSENZA

*cattan-**zar**-ro*
CATANZARO

*pal-**lair**-mo*
PALERMO

*mess-**see**-na*
MESSINA

SICILY
*see-**cheel**-ya*
SICILIA

red-jo
REGGIO

*ka-**tan**-ya*
CATÁNIA

ra-goo-sah
RAGUSA

*see-ra-**koo**-zay*
SYRACUSE

AUSTRALIA
ow-stra-leeya
AUSTRALIA

Cairns
Townsville
Mackay
Rockhampton
Brisbane
Grafton
Newcastle
Sydney
Canberra
Albury
Melbourne
Adelaide
Alice Springs
Darwin
Perth

TASMANIA
Hobart

NEW ZEALAND
nvor-va tsay-lan-da
NUOVA ZELANDA

NORTH ISLAND
Gisborne
Napier
Wellington
Auckland
Hamilton
New Plymouth
Blenheim
Nelson
Greymouth
Christchurch
SOUTH ISLAND
Dunedin
Invercargill

ENGLAND
eenghel-tair-ra
INGHILTERRA

SCOTLAND
skot-seeya
SCOZIA

Elgin
Inverness
Aberdeen
Montrose
Dundee
Perth
Stirling
Edinburgh
Glasgow
Ayr
Dumfries
Stranraer
Isle of Skye

Berwick
Newcastle
Carlisle
Darlington
Middlesbrough
Lancaster
Preston
Liverpool
Isle of Man

York
Hull
Leeds
Manchester
Sheffield
Chester
Stoke
Derby
Nottingham
Lincoln
Leicester
Peterborough
Northampton
Norwich
Cambridge
Ipswich
Felixstowe
Bedford
Coventry
Birmingham
Oxford
London
Gloucester
Reading
Brighton
Southampton
Bristol
Bath
Salisbury
Bournemouth
Exeter
Weymouth
Plymouth
Dover
Folkestone
Portsmouth

Shrewsbury

WALES
ga-less
GALLES

Bangor
Holyhead
Aberystwyth
Fishguard
Swansea
Newport
Cardiff

NORTHERN IRELAND
eer-lan-da del nord
IRLANDA DEL NORD

Londonderry
Belfast

IRELAND
eer-lan-da
IRLANDA

Dublin
Wexford
Waterford
Galway
Limerick
Cork

St. John's

NEWFOUNDLAND

Halifax

St. John

Quebec

Montreal

Ottawa

Providence

LONG I

Boston

New York

Buffalo

Philadelphia

Baltimore

Washington D.C.

Charlotte

BAHAMAS

Miami

Toronto

Detroit

Cleveland

Pittsburg

Cincinnati

Louisville

Nashville

Chattanooga

Atlanta

Jacksonville

Tampa

HUDSON BAY

CANADA
kann-a-dah
CANADA

Minneapolis ● St Paul

Milwaukee

Chicago

Indianapolis

St. Louis

Memphis

Birmingham

Mobile

Jackson

New Orleans

Winnipeg

Des Moines

Omaha

Kansas City

Edmonton

Calgary

Saskatoon

Regina

UNITED STATES
star-tee oo-nee-tee
STATI UNITI

Wichita

Oklahoma City

Dallas

Houston

San Antonio

MEXICO

Anchorage

Denver

Salt Lake City

Albuquerque

Las Vegas

Phoenix

Tuscon

El Paso

Vancouver

Seattle

Portland

Eugene

Los Angeles

San Diego

San Fransisco

VANCOUVER I

?

I	*ee-yo* **IO**	would like	*vor-ray-ee* **VORREI**
my	*eel mee-yo* **IL MIO**	want	*vwar-lay* **VUOLE**
he	*lwee* **LUI**	have	*oh* **HO**
she	*lay-ee* **LEI**	have	*ah* **HA**
his	*eel soo-oh* **IL SUO**	do you have	*ah-vet-tay* **AVETE**
her	*la soo-ah* **LA SUA**	can I	*poss-o* **POSSO**
we	*noy* **NOI**	can I have	*poss-o ah-vair-ray* **POSSO AVERE**
us	*noy* **NOI**	can you	*pwoh* **PUÒ**
our	*noss-tro* **NOSTRO**		
you	*lay-ee* **LEI**		
your	*eel soo-oh* **IL SUO**		

am	*so-no* **SONO**
is	*eh* **È**
are	*so-no* **SONO**
Change	*cambee-yar-ray* **CAMBIARE**
Come back	*tor-nar-ray* **TORNARE**
Feed	*alla-tar-ray* **ALLATTARE**
Go	*an-dar-ray* **ANDARE**
Play	*joc-kar-ray* **GIOCARE**

who	*kee* **CHI**	born	*nar-toh* **NATO**
		died	*mor-toh* **MORTO**
not	*non* **NON**	older	*pee-yoo vec-keeyo* **PIÙ VECCHIO**
no	*non* **NON**	younger	*pee-yoo jo-var-nay* **PIÙ GIOVANE**

19
1 1
2 2
3 3
4 4
5 5
6 6
7 7
8 8
9 9

which	*kwar-lay* **QUALE**	same age	*stay-sa et-ta* **STESSA ETÀ**
where	*doh-vay* **DOVE**	single	*non sposs-star-toh* **NON SPOSATO**
when	*kwan-doh* **QUANDO**	married	*sposs-sar-toh* **SPOSATO**
what	*koh-sa* **COSA**	divorced	*deevortsee-yar-toh* **DIVORZIATO**

name	*no-may* **NOME**
address	*eendee-reet-so* **INDIRIZZO**
phone no	*noo-mairo dee tel-lef-onno* **Nº DI TELEFONO**

what time	*kay or-ra* **CHE ORA**	at *al* **AL**	by *ah* **A**	for *pair* **PER**	from *dah* **DA**	in *een* **IN**	to *ah* **A**	with *con* **CON**
how old	*kwan-tee ar-nee* **QUANTI ANNI**						

husband	*ma-**ree**-toh* **MARITO**		boy	*rag-**gat**-so* **RAGAZZO**
wife	***mol**-yay* **MOGLIE**		girl	*rag-**gat**-sa* **RAGAZZA**
			man	***woh**-mo* **UOMO**
father	***par**-dray* **PADRE**		woman	***don**-na* **DONNA**
mother	***mar**-dray* **MADRE**		boyfriend	*rag-**gat**-so* **RAGAZZO**
baby	***beem**-bo* **BIMBO**		girlfriend	*rag-**gat**-sa* **RAGAZZA**
child	*bam-**bee**-no* **BAMBINO**		fiancè (m)	*feedan-**tsar**-toh* **FIDANZATO**
children	*bam-**bee**-nee* **BAMBINI**		fiancè (f)	*feedan-**tsar**-ta* **FIDANZATA**
			friend	*am-**mee**-ko* **AMICO**
son	***feel**-yo* **FIGLIO**		colleague	*col-**lay**-ga* **COLLEGA**
daughter	***feel**-ya* **FIGLIA**			
brother	*fra-**tel**-lo* **FRATELLO**		babysitter	*babysitter* **BABYSITTER**
sister	*sor-**rel**-la* **SORELLA**		bedtime	***or**-ray dee corree-**car**-see* **ORA DI CORICARSI**
grandfather	***non**-no* **NONNO**		(warm) bottle	*(reescal-**dar**-ray) bee-bairron* **(RISCALDARE) BIBERON**
grandmother	***non**-na* **NONNAH**		cot/crib	*let-**tee**-no* **LETTINO**
grandson	*nee-**po**-tay* **NIPOTE**		diaper/nappy	*panno-**lee**-no* **PANNOLINO**
grand-daughter	*nee-**po**-tay* **NIPOTE**		high chair	*sedjo-**lo**-nay* **SEGGIOLONE**
uncle	***tsee**-yo* **ZIO**		creche	*a-**see**-lo* **ASILO**
aunt	***tsee**-ya* **ZIA**		paddling pool	*pee-**shee**-na pair bam-**bee**-no* **PISCINA PER BAMBINO**
newphew	*nee-**po**-tay* **NIPOTE**		playground	***cam**-po **joc**-kee* **CAMPO GIOCHI**
niece	*nee-**po**-tay* **NIPOTE**		anything for children to do	***too**-toh pair ockoo-**par**-ray ee bam-**bee**-nee* **TUTTO PER OCCUPARE I BAMBINI**
cousin	*coo-**jee**-no* **CUGINO**			

? I *ee-yo* **IO**

my *eel **mee**-yo* **IL MIO**

he *lwee* **LUI**

she *lay-ee* **LEI**

we *noy* **NOI**

us *noy* **NOI**

you *lay-ee* **LEI**

not *non* **NON**

no *non* **NON**

which *kwar-lay* **QUALE**

where *doh-vay* **DOVE**

when *kwan-doh* **QUANDO**

what *koh-sa* **COSA**

what time *kay or-ra* **CHE ORA**

how *koh-may* **COME**

how long *kwan-toh tem-po* **QUANTO TEMPO**

how many *kwan-tee* **QUANTI**

would like	*vor-**ray**-ee* **VORREI**	
would like	*vor-**ray**-mo* **VORREMMO**	
want	*vwar-lay* **VUOLE**	
have	*oh* **HO**	
have	*abbee-**yar**-mo* **ABBIAMO**	
have	*ah* **HA**	
do you have	*ah-**vet**-tay* **AVETE**	
can I	*poss-o* **POSSO**	
can I have	*poss-o ah-**vair**-ray* **POSSO AVERE**	
can we	*possee-**yar**-mo* **POSSIAMO**	
can we have	*possee-**yar**-mo ah-**vair**-ray* **POSSIAMO AVERE**	

can you *pwoh* **PUÒ**

is *eh* **È**

are *so-no* **SONO**

Change *cambee-**yar**-ray* **CAMBIARE**

Cook *kwoh-chair-ray* **CUOCERE**

Eat *man-**jar**-ray* **MANGIARE**

Order *ordee-**nar**-ray* **ORDINARE**

Recommend *conseel-**yar**-ray* **CONSIGLIARE**

Reserve *reezair-**var**-ray* **RISERVARE**

See *ved-**dair**-ray* **VEDERE**

Wait *aspet-**tar**-ray* **ASPETTARE**

table *tar-volo* **TAVOLO**

person *pair-so-na* **PERSONA**

meal *pas-toh* **PASTO**

snack *spoon-**tee**-no* **SPUNTINO**

lunch *colatsee-yo-nay* **COLAZIONE**

dinner *chen-na* **CENA**

open *a-**pair**-toh* **APERTO**

closed *kee-oo-zo* **CHIUSO**

now *a-**dess**-o* **ADESSO**

earlier *pee-yoo press-toh* **PIÙ PRESTO**

later *pee-yoo tar-dee* **PIÙ TARDI**

toilet *toy-**let**-tay* **TOILETTE**

near *vee-**chee**-no* **VICINO**

here *kwee* **QUI**

there *lar* **LÀ**

HOW MUCH IS (THAT)? *kwan-toh coss-ta* **QUANTO COSTA?**

and	at	for	in	more	too	with
ay **E**	*al* **AL**	*pair* **PER**	*een* **IN**	*pee-yoo* **PIÙ**	*trop-po* **TROPPO**	*con* **CON**

			EATING PLACES
by window	*vee-**chee**-no alla fee-**ness**-tra* **VICINO ALLA FINESTRA**		
outside	*alla-**pair**-toh* **ALL'APERTO**	**AUTOGRILL** *owtoh-grill*	A motorway restaurant and cafeteria.
chair	*say-deeya* **SEDIA**	**BAR** *bar*	A Bar. Usually also serve coffee. "Tavola Calda" means hot bar-snacks are available.
menu	*men-**noo*** **MENÙ**	**CAFFÈ** *caf-**fay***	A coffee shop. Usually also serve breakfast.
set menu	*men-**noo** fee-so* **MENÙ FISSO**	**OSTERIA** *Ostair-ree-ya*	An Inn. Usually serve simple food.
wine list	***leess**-ta day vee-nee* **LISTA DEI VINI**	**PIZZERIA** *peetsair-ree-ya*	A Pizza parlour.
some	*del* **DEL**	**RISTORANTE** *reestor-**ran**-tay*	A good class of restaurant. varying standards and classifications.
something	*kwal-**co**-sa* **QUALCOSA**	**ROSTICCERIA** *rosteechair-ree-ya*	A shop/snack bar specialising in grilled meats and fish.
light (food)	*led-**jair**-ro* **LEGGERO**	**TRATTORIA** *trattor-ree-ya*	A medium-priced restaurant.
vegetarian	*vegetaree-**yar**-no* **VEGETARIANO**	**TAVERNA** *ta-**vair**-na*	A cheap restaurant.
local dish	*pee-**yar**-tee lo-**car**-lee* **PIATTI LOCALI**	CONDIMENTS ETC 28A	**CONDIMENTI**
hot	*cal-doh* **CALDO**	BREAKFAST 28A	**COLAZIONE**
cold	*fray-doh* **FREDDO**	APPETIZER 28B	**ANTIPASTO**
		SOUP 28B	**ZUPPA**
hot (spicy)	*sappor-**ree**-toh* **SAPORITO**	MEAT 29A	**CARNE**
		GAME 29A	**SELVAGGINA**
fresh	*fres-co* **FRESCO**	POULTRY 29A	**POLLAME**
		FISH 29A	**PESCE**
		PASTA 30A	**PASTA**
large	*gran-day* **GRANDE**	PIZZA 30A	**PIZZA**
		EGGS 30A	**UOVA**
small	*pee-ko-lo* **PICCOLO**	RICE 30A	**RISO**
		VEGETABLES 30B	**VERDURA**
portion	*portsee-yo-nay* **PORZIONE**	CHEESE 31A	**FORMAGGIO**
		DESSERT 31A	**DESSERT**
another	*oon al-tro* **UN ALTRO**	FRUIT 31B	**FRUTTA**
		SOFT DRINKS 31B	**BIBITA ANALCOLICA**
		TEA & COFFEE 31B	**TÈ & CAFFÈ**
waiter	*cammairee-**yair**-ray* **CAMERIERE**	ALCOHOLIC DRINKS 32A	**BIBITA ALCOLICA**
		SNACKS 32B	**SPUNTINO**
waitress	*cammairee-**yair**-ra* **CAMERIERA**	PAYING 32B	**PAGAMENTO CONTO**

the following pages are indicated above

CONDIMENTS ETC				BREAKFAST	*colatsee-yo-nay* **COLAZIONE**		
Bread	*par-nay* **PANE**	(rolls)	*(par-nee-nee)* **(PANINI)**	Fruit juice	*soo-ko dee froo-ta* **SUCCO DI FRUTTA**		
Butter	*boo-ro* **BURRO**			Cereal	*fee-yoc-kee dar-ven-nah* **FIOCCHI D'AVENA**		
Dressing	*condee-men-toh* **CONDIMENTO**			Boiled egg	*woh-vo alla cock* **UOVO ALLA COQUE**		
Honey	*mee-yel-lay* **MIELE**			(soft/medium/hard)	*(mol-lay/met-so /so-doh)* **MOLLE MEZZO SODO)**		
Lemon	*lee-mo-nay* **LIMONE**	(juice of)	*(soo-ko dee)* **(SUCCO DI)**	Fried egg	*woh-vo free-toh* **UOVO FRITTO**		
Margarine	*margar-ree-na* **MARGARINA**			Poached egg	*woh-vo cam-mee-cha* **UOVO CAMICIA**		
Mustard	*say-nappay* **SENAPE**			Scrambled egg	*woh-va strappat-sar-tay* **UOVA STRAPAZZATE**		
Oil	*ol-yo* **OLIO**			Omlette	*free-tar-ta* **FRITTATA**		
Salt & pepper	*sar-lay ay pay-pay* **SALE E PEPE**			Pancake	*free-tar-ta* **FRITTATA**		
Sauce (tomato)	*sal-sa (pommee-dor-ro)* **SALSA (POMIDORO)**			Bacon & egg	*woh-vo ay pan-chet-ta* **UOVO E PANCETTA**		
Sugar	*tsoo-kairo* **ZUCCHERO**			Ham & egg	*pror-shoo-toh ay woh-vo* **PROSCIUTTO E UOVO**		
Vingegar	*at-chet-toh* **ACETO**			Toast	*toast* **TOAST**		
Water	*ak-wa* **ACQUA**			(an Italian crisp bun)	*bree-yosh* **BRIOCHES**		
				(an Italian flaky pastry)	*foc-kat-cheeya* **FOCACCIA**		
Knife	*col-tel-lo* **COLTELLO**			Jam	*marmel-lar-tah* **MARMELLATA**		
Fork	*for-ket-ta* **FORCHETTA**			Marmalade	*marmel-lar-tah* **MARMELLATA**		
Spoon	*koo-keeya-oh* **CUCCHIAIO**			Yoghurt	*ee-yor-goort* **YOGURT**		
Ashtray	*porta-chen-nair-ray* **PORTACENERE**						
Cup	*tat-sa* **TAZZA**	a	*oon* **UN**				
Glass	*beekee-yair-ray* **BICCHIERE**	some	*del* **DEL**	Coffee	*caf-fay* **CAFFÉ**	Tea	*tay* **TÉ**
Napkin	*tovarlee-yor-lo* **TOVAGLIOLO**	hot	*cal-doh* **CALDO**	Cream	*par-na* **PANNA**	Lemon	*lee-mo-nay* **LIMONE**
Plate	*pee-yar-toh* **PIATTO**	cold	*fray-doh* **FREDDO**	Milk	*lar-tay* **LATTE**		

paying: 32B   other soft drinks: 31B   fruits/frutti: 31B

APPETIZER	*antee-**pass**-toh* **ANTIPASTO**		APPETIZER TYPES	*tee-pee de antee-**pass**-toh* **TIPI DI ANTIPASTO**
avocado	*avo-**car**-doh* **AVOCADO**		Cheese	*for-**mar**-jo* **FORMAGGIO**
anchovies	*at-**choo**-gay* **ACCIUGHE**		Egg	*woh-vo* **UOVO**
pork cold cuts	*affet-**tar**-tee mee-stee* **AFFETTATI MISTI**		Fish	*pesh-ay* **PESCE**
mixed appetizer	*antee-**pass**-toh mees-toh* **ANTIPASTO MISTO**		Fruit	*froo-ta* **FRUTTA**
artichoke	*car-**cho**-fee* **CARCIOFI**		Fruit juice	*soo-ko dee froo-ta* **SUCCO DI FRUTTA**
raw vegetables & hot sauce	***ban**-ya **kow**-da* **BAGNA CAUDA**		Meat	*car-nay* **CARNE**
caviar	*carvee-**yar**-lay* **CAVIALE**		Pasta	*pass-ta* **PASTA**
smoked pork	*koola-**tel**-lo* **CULATELLO**		Salad	*eensal-**lar**-ta* **INSALATA**
mixed seafood	***froo**-tee dee **mar**-ray* **FRUTTI DI MARE**		Vegetable	*vair-**doo**-ra* **VERDURA**
shrimps	*gambair-**ret**-tee* **GAMBERETTI**			
prawns	***gam**-bair-ree* **GAMBERI**		SOUP	*tsoo-pa* **ZUPPA**
Bologna sausage	*morta-**del**-la* **MORTADELLA**		broth	*bror-**det**-toh* **BRODETTO**
Olives	*ol-**lee**-vay* **OLIVE**		bouillion	*bror-doh* **BRODO**
(stuffed)	*(far-**chee**-tay)* **(FARCITE)**		fish stew	*boo-**ree**-dah* **BURIDDA**
(black/green)	*(**nair**-ray/**vair**-dee)* **(NERE VERDI)**		spicy tripe stew	*boo-**zec**-ka* **BUSECCA**
oysters	*oss-treekay* **OSTRICHE**		a spicy seafood stew	*kat-**choo**-ko* **CACCIUCCO**
ham	*pror-**shoo**-toh* **PROSCIUTTO**		thick veg. soup	*meeness-**tro**-nay* **MINESTRONE**
(smoked)	*(affoomee-**car**-toh)* **(AFFUMICATO)**		vegetable soup	*pas-**sar**-toh dee vair-**doo**-ra* **PASSATO DI VERDURA**
(cooked/cured)	*(**kot**-toh/**croo**-doh)* **(COTTO CRUDO)**		rice & pea soup	***ree**-see ay **bee**-see* **RISI E BISI**
(wild boar)	*dee cheeng-**yar**-lay)* **(DI CINGHIALE)**		egg consommé	*stratcha-**tel**-la* **STRACCIATELLA**
salami	*sal-**lar**-may* **SALAME**		vegetable wine & noodle soup	*tsoo-pa alla ven-**net**-ah* **ZUPPA ALLA VENETA**
white truffles	*tar-**too**-fee* **TARTUFI**		cold soup	*tsoo-pa **fray**-da* **ZUPPA FREDDA**

meat & fish/carne & pesce: 29A   **vegetables/verdura: 30B**   **pasta: 30A**

MEAT	*car-nay* **CARNE**	GAME	*selva-jee-na* **SELVAGGINA**	FISH	*pesh-ay* **PESCE**
lamb	*an-yel-lo* **AGNELLO**	kid goat	*cap-pret-toh* **CAPRETTO**	anchovies	*a-choo-gay* **ACCIUGHE**
pork	*my-yar-lay* **MAIALE**	roebuck	*cappree-yo-lo* **CAPRIOLO**	eel	*ang-gwee-la* **ANGUILLA**
beef	*mant-so* **MANZO**	deer	*chair-vo* **CERVO**	lobster	*arra-goss-ta* **ARAGOSTA**
mutton	*mon-toh-nay* **MONTONE**	wild boar	*cheeghee-yar-lay* **CINGHIALE**	herring	*ar-reeng-gah* **ARINGA**
bacon	*pan-chet-ta* **PANCETTA**	rabbit	*con-neel-yo* **CONIGLIO**	scallops	*ar-sel-lay* **ARSELLE**
ham	*pror-shoo-toh* **PROSCIUTTO**	hare	*lep-ray* **LEPRE**	dried cod	*backar-lah* **BACCALÀ**
sausages	*sal-see-chay* **SALSICCE**	venison	*selva-jee-na* **SELVAGGINA**	whitebait	*beeyang-ket-tee* **BIANCHETTI**
veal	*vee-tel-lo* **VITELLO**			sea bass	*brant-see-no* **BRANZINO**
		POULTRY	*pol-lar-may* **POLLAME**	baby squid	*callamar-ret-tee* **CALAMARETTI**
steak	*bees-tec-ka* **BISTECCA**	lark	*al-loh-doh-la* **ALLODOLA**	squid	*calla-mar-ree* **CALAMARI**
chop	*brat-cho-la* **BRACIOLA**	duck	*ar-neetra* **ANITRA**	carp	*car-pa* **CARPA**
rib	*koss-toh-la* **COSTOLA**	woodcock	*bec-kat-cha* **BECCACCIA**	mussels	*coat-say* **COZZE**
cutlet	*costo-let-ta* **COSTOLETTA**	pheasant	*fa-jar-no* **FAGIANO**	shrimps	*gambair-ret-tee* **GAMBERETTI**
liver	*feg-gartoh* **FEGATO**	guinea fowl	*farra-oh-na* **FARAONA**	prawns	*gam-bair-ree* **GAMBERI**
fillet	*fee-let-toh* **FILETTO**	grouse	*gar-lo ched-ro-ay* **GALLO CEDRONE**	crabs	*grang-keeyo* **GRANCHIO**
tongue	*leeng-gwa* **LINGUA**	goose	*oc-ka* **OCA**	conger eel	*grong-ghee* **GRONGHI**
loin	*lom-bo* **LOMBO**	partridge	*pair-nee-chay* **PERNICE**	lamprey	*lam-pray-day* **LAMPREDE**
marrow	*mee-doh-lo* **MIDOLLO**	pigeon	*pee-cho-nay* **PICCIONE**	pike	*loo-cho* **LUCCIO**
meatballs	*pol-pet-tay* **POLPETTE**	plover	*peevee-yair-ray* **PIVIERE**	sea snails	*loo-mac-kay di mar-ray* **LUMACHE DI MARE**
kidneys	*ron-yo-nee* **ROGNONI**	chicken	*pol-lo* **POLLO**	whiting	*mair-lar-no* **MERLANO**
escallop	*scalo-pee-na* **SCALOPPINA**	quail	*kwar-lyah* **QUAGLIA**	cod	*mair-loot-so* **MERLUZZO**
tripe	*tree-pay* **TRIPPE**	turkey	*tac-kee-no* **TACCHINO**	oysters	*oss-treekay* **OSTRICHE**

vegetables/verdura: 30B   cheese/formaggio: 31A   herbs/erbe: 35B

COOKING METHODS *moh*-doh dee *kwoh*-chair-ray
MODO DI CUOCERE

plaice	*passair-ree-no* **PASSERINO**	poached	*affogar-toh* **AFFOGATO**
perch	*pesh-ay pair-seeko* **PESCE PERSICO**	smoked	*affoomee-kar-toh* **AFFUMICATO**
swordfish	*pesh-ay spar-da* **PESCE SPADA**	roasted	*arross-tee-toh* **ARROSTITO**
plaice	*peeya-noot-sa* **PIANUZZA**	deep fried	*bain free-toh* **BEN FRITTO**
octopus	*pol-po* **POLPO**	braised	*bras-sar-toh* **BRASATO**
ray	*rat-sa* **RAZZA**	steamed	*cot-toh ah vap-por-ray* **COTTO A VAPORE**
sea urchins	*ree-chee* **RICCI**	casseroled	*een cassair-woo-la* **IN CASSEROLA**
turbot	*rom-bo* **ROMBO**	stuffed	*far-chee-toh* **FARCITO**
salmon	*sal-moh-nay* **SALMONE**	baked	*al for-no* **AL FORNO**
John Dory	*san pee-yet-ro* **SAN PIETRO**	fried	*free-toh* **FRITTO**
sardines	*sar-dee-nay* **SARDINE**	barbecued	*alla gra-tee-ko-la* **ALLA GRATICOLA**
prawns	*scam-pee* **SCAMPI**	grilled	*al-la greel-ya* **ALLA GRIGLIA**
sea scorpion	*scor-farno* **SCORFANO**	boiled	*less-oh* **LESSO**
mackerel	*zgom-bro* **SGOMBRO**	broiled	*al-lo spee-yay-doh* **ALLO SPIEDO**
cuttlefish	*sep-peeya* **SEPPIA**	stewed	*een oo-meedo* **IN UMIDO**
sole	*sor-leeyo-la* **SOGLIOLA**		
sea bass	*spee-go-la* **SPIGOLA**	rare	*al sang-gway* **AL SANGUE**
sturgeon	*storee-yo-nay* **STORIONE**	medium	*ah poon-tee-no* **A PUNTINO**
tuna	*ton-no* **TONNO**	well-done	*bain cot-toh* **BEN COTTO**
red mullet	*treel-yay* **TRIGLIE**		
trout	*trot-ta* **TROTA**	with	*con* **CON**
clams	*vong-go-lay* **VONGOLE**	herbs	*air-bay* **ERBE**
		sauce	*sal-sa* **SALSA**

pas-ta **PASTA**	PASTA Flour-based specialities, eg. spaghetti, macaroni, noodles, ravioli; eaten alone, with soups or with meals or forming part of special dishes.		*peet*-sa **PIZZA**	PIZZA
			kapree-cho-sa **CAPRICCIOSA**	chef's speciality
			calt-so-nay **CALZONE**	folded over like a pancake, – cheeses ham & tomatoes
annyo-lot-tee **AGNOLOTTI**	A type of ravioli with savoury meat, vegetables, herbs and garlic.		*froo-tee dee mar*-ray **FRUTTI DI MARE**	seafood
can-ned-dairlee **CANEDERLI**	Dumplings with ham sausage & breadcrumbs.		*margair-ree*-ta **MARGHERITA**	tomato, mozzarella cheese and basil.
cappel-let-tee **CAPPELLETTI**	Small ravioli with meat, herbs, cheese and eggs.		*napolee-tar*-na **NAPOLITANA**	anchovies, oregano, ham, cheese, capers and tomato
fettoo-chee-nay **FETTUCCINE**	Flat narrow noodles		*seecheelee-yar*-na **SICILIANA**	black cheese and capers
la-san-yay **LASAGNE**	Alternating layers of pasta with tomato, sausage ham, cheese & white sauce.		*peet-set*-ta **PIZZETTA**	small pizza
maka-ro-nee **MACCHERONI**	Macaroni		**PIZZA RUSTICA**	(see pasta dishes)
pantsar-rot-tee **PANZAROTTI**	Dough filled with pork, eggs, cheese & anchovies.			
pappar-del-lay **PAPPARDELLE**	Long wide noodles			
peet-sa *roos*-teeka **PIZZA RUSTICA**	Pasta pie with sausage, egg, cheese and vegetables.		EGGS *woh*-va **UOVA**	
spa-ghet-ti **SPAGHETTI**	Spaghetti		omlet (with) *free-tar*-ta *(con)* **FRITTATA (CON)**	
tajeeya-tel-lay **TAGLIATELLE**	Flat noodles.		thin omlet with cheese & cream *freeta-tee*-nay *peeyaymon-tess*-see **FRITTATINE PIEMONTESI**	
tortel-lee-nee **TORTELLINI**	Rings of dough with seasoned mincemeat		pancake *free-tel*-la **FRITTELLA**	
			boiled egg *woh*-vo alla *cock* **UOVO ALLA COQUE**	
ree-so **RISO**	RICE		(soft/medium/hard) *(mol*-lay/*met*-so /*so*-doh) **MOLLE MEZZO SODO**	
ree-so een *bee-yang*-ko **RISO IN BIANCO**	Boiled rice with parmesan cheese		fried egg *woh*-vo *free*-toh **UOVO FRITTO**	
ree-sot-toh **RISOTTO**	Rice casserole		poached egg *woh*-vo *cam-mee*-cha **UOVO CAMICIA**	
			scrambled egg *woh*-vo *strappat-sar*-toh **UOVO STRAPPAZZATO**	

meat & fish/carne & pesce: 29   cheese/formaggio: 31A   herbs/erbe: 35B

VEGETABLES & SALADS	*vair-**doo**-ra ay eensal-**lar**-ta* **VERDURA & ENSALATA**	parsnips	*pastee-**nar**-ka* **PASTINACA**
Asparagus	*ass-**par**-rarjee* **ASPARAGI**	peppers/pimentoes	*peppair-**ro**-nee* **PEPERONI**
avocado	*avo-**car**-doh* **AVOCADO**	peas	*pee-**sel**-lee* **PISELLI**
beetroot	*barbarbee-**yet**-toh-lay* **BARBABIETOLE**	tomatoes	*pommee-**dor**-ro* **POMIDORO**
artichoke	*car-**chof**-fee* **CARCIOFI**	leeks	*por-ree* **PORRI**
carrots	*car-**rot**-tay* **CAROTE**	turnips	*rar-pay* **RAPE**
cauliflower	*kavolfee-**yor**-ray* **CAVOLFIORE**	radishes	*ravva-**nel**-lee* **RAVANELLI**
cabbage	***kav**-volee* **CAVOLI**	rice (Boiled)	***ree**-so (een bee-**yang**-ko)* **RISO (IN BIANCO)**
Brussels Sprouts	*kavvo-**lee**-nee dee broo-**sail*** **CAVOLINI DI BRUXELLES**	celery	***sed**-darno* **SEDANO**
cucumbers	*chetree-**yo**-lee* **CETRIOLI**	spinach	*spee-**nar**-chee* **SPINACI**
gherkins	*chetreeyo-**lee**-nee* **CETRIOLINI**	truffles	*tar-**too**-fee* **TARTUFI**
onions	*chee-**po**-lay* **CIPOLLE**	fresh vegetables	*vair-**doo**-ra **fress**-ka* **VERDURA FRESCA**
French beans	*fadjo-**lee**-nee* **FAGIOLINI**	mixed vegetables	*vair-**doo**-ra **meess**-ta* **VERDURA MISTA**
runner beans	*fadjo-**lee**-nee* **FAGIOLINI**	green cabbage	***vairt**-sa* **VERZA**
broad beans	***far**-vay* **FAVE**	ginger	***tsent**-sairo* **ZENZERO**
mushrooms	***foong**-ghee* **FUNGHI**	marrow/pumpkin	***tsoo**-ka* **ZUCCA**
salad	*eensal-**lar**-ta* **INSALATA**	courgettes/zucchini	*tsoo-**kee**-nee* **ZUCCHINI**
mixed salad	*eensal-**lar**-ta **meess**-ta* **INSALATA MISTA**		
green salad	*ensal-**lar**-ta **vair**-day* **INSALATA VERDE**	POTATOES	*pat-**tat**-ay* **PATATE**
lettuce	*lat-**too**-ga* **LATTUGA**	(boiled)	*less-say* **LESSE**
lentils	*len-tee-keeyay* **LENTICCHIE**	(croquette)	*cro-**ket**-tay* **CROCCHETTE**
sweetcorn	***mah**-ees **dol**-chay* **MAIS DOLCE**	(jacket)	*kon boo-**chee**-ya* **CON BUCCIA**
aubergine	*melant-**sar**-nay* **MELANZANE**	(chips french fried)	*pattat-**tee**-nay freetay* **PATATINE FRITTE**

(mashed)	*poo-**ray*** **PURÈ**		
(roast)	*ar-**ross**-tay* **ARROSTE**		
(sauté)	*sal-**tar**-tay* **SALTATE**		

*for-**mar**-jo* **FORMAGGIO**	CHEESE	

*for-**mar**-jee dol-chee* **FORMAGGI DOLCI**	MILD CHEESES
*bel pa-**ay**-zay* **BEL PAESE**	soft & mild
*fon-**tee**-na* **FONTINA**	fat & creamy
*dol-chay **lar**-tay* **DOLCE LATTE**	mild blue cheese
***grar**-na* **GRANA**	parmesan cheese
*mascar-**po**-nay* **MASCARPONE**	very creamy
*parmee-**jar**-no red-**jar**-no* **PARMIGIANO REGGIANO**	parmesan cheese
*provva-**too**-ra* **PROVATURA**	soft, mild & slightly sweet
*raggoo-**sar**-no* **RAGUSANO**	hard & slightly sweet
*scam-**mort**-sa* **SCAMORZA**	soft, sweet & salty
*strac-**kee**-no* **STRACCHINO**	soft & fatty

*for-**mar**-jee pee-**can**-tee* **FORMAGGI PICCANTI**	SHARP CHEESES
*ass-**see**-yargo* **ASIAGO**	
*gorgon-**zoh**-la* **GORGONZOLA**	strong blue cheese
*provvo-**lo**-nay* **PROVOLONE**	hard & tangy

*al-tree for-**mar**-jee* **ALTRI FORMAGGI**	OTHER CHEESES
*kat-**chee**-yo ka-**val**-lo* **CACIOCAVALLO**	sweet cheese
*motsar-**rel**-la* **MOZZARELLA**	soft sweet buffalo milk cheese
*peckor-**ree**-no* **PECORINO**	ewe's milk cheese
*ree-**cot**-ta* **RICOTTA**	ewe's milk cheese

a (small) piece of	*oon **pet**-so (**pee**-ko-lo)* **UN PEZZO (PICCOLO)**
some/something	*del /kwal-**co**-sa* **DEL QUALCOSA**
not too sweet	*non **trop**-po dol-chay* **NON TROPPO DOLCE**
with	*con* **CON**

DESSERT	*dessert* **DESSERT**
pudding	*boo-**dee**-no* **BUDINO**
ice cream & crystalised fruit	*cass-**sar**-ta* **CASSATA**
rich ice cream cake	*cass-**sar**-ta seecheelee-**yar**-na* **CASSATA SICILIANA**
cake	*dol-chay/**tor**-ta* **DOLCE TORTA**
ice cream	*jel-**lar**-toh* **GELATO**
water ice	*gran-**nee**-ta* **GRANITA**
a creamy cheese	*mascar-**po**-ay* **MASCARPONE**
a spicy sugar cake	*pan-**for**-tay* **PANFORTE**
a spicy sultana bun	*panet-**toh**-nay* **PANETTONE**
pastry	*pastee-**chee**-no* **PASTICCINO**
nougat	*tor-**ro**-nay* **TORRONE**
a type of trifle	*tsoo-pa eeng-**glay**-zay* **ZUPPA INGLESE**
cream	***par**-na* **PANNA**
sauce	*sal-sa* **SALSA**
sugar	*tsoo-kairo* **ZUCCHERO**

FRUIT	*froo*-ta **FRUTTA**	SOFT DRINKS, TEA & COFFEE	bee-**bee**-tay, tay & caf-**fay** **BIBITE, TÈ & CAFFÈ**
apricot	albee-**cok**-kah **ALBICOCCA**	Chocolate	choco-**lar**-toh **CIOCCOLATO**
pineapple	anna-**nass** **ANANAS**	Coffee	caf-**fay** **CAFFÈ**
watermelon	ang-**goo**-reeya **ANGURIA**	(expresso coffee)	(caf-**fay** ess-**press**-so) **(CAFFÈ ESPRESSO)**
orange	ar-**ran**-cha **ARANCIA**	(expresso + chocolate)	(cappoo-**chee**-no) **(CAPPUCCINO)**
bananas	bar-**nar**-nay **BANANE**	(iced coffee)	(caf-**fay** **fray**-doh) **(CAFFÈ FREDDO)**
lime	**ched**-ro **CEDRO**	(weaker expresso)	(caf-**fay** **loong**-go) **(CAFFÈ LUNGO)**
cherries	cheelee-**ay**-jay **CILIEGE**	(strong expresso)	(rees-**tret**-toh) **(RISTRETTO)**
figs	*fee*-kee **FICHI**	(with cream)	(con **par**-na) **(CON PANNA)**
strawberries	*frar*-go-lay **FRAGOLE**	Fruit juice	*soo*-ko dee *froo*-ta **SUCCO DI FRUTTA**
raspberries	*lam*-po-nee **LAMPONI**	Lemonade	leemo-**nar**-ta **LIMONATA**
lemon	lee-**mo**-nay **LIMONE**	Milk	**lar**-tay **LATTÈ**
tangerine	mandar-**ree**-nee **MANDARINI**	Milkshake	froo-**lar**-toh dee **lar**-tay **FRULLATO DI LATTE**
apple	**mel**-la **MELA**	Mineral water	akwa meenair-**rar**-lay **ACQUA MINERALE**
melon	mel-**lo**-nay **MELONE**	Orangeade	arran-**char**-ta **ARANCIATA**
blackberries	**mor**-ray **MORE**	Soda water	seltz **SELZ**
nuts	**not**-chee **NOCI**	Squash (fruit drink)	spray-**moo**-ta **SPREMUTA**
pear	**pair**-ra **PERA**	Tea	tay **TÈ**
peach	**pes**-ka **PESCA**	(iced tea)	(tay **fray**-doh) **(TÈ FREDDO)**
grapefruit	pom-**pell**-mo **POMPELMO**	(with milk)	(con **lar**-tay) **(CON LATTÈ)**
plum	**proon**-ya **PRUGNA**	(sugar/lemon)	(tsoo-kairo/lee-**mo**-nay) **(ZUCCHERO LIMONE)**
prune	**proon**-ya **sec**-ka **PRUGNA SECCA**	Tonic water	**ak**-wa **ton**-neeka **ACQUA TONICA**
grapes	*oo*-va **UVA**	(glass of) Water	(beekee-**yair**-ray dee) **ak**-wa **(BICCHIERE DI) ACQUA**

alcoholic drinks: 32A   paying: 32B

ALCOHOLIC DRINKS	*bee-beetay alcoo-lee-kay* **BIBITE ALCOOLICHE**		Carafe	*car-raf-fa* **CARAFFA**
Aperitif	*apairee-tee-vo* **APERITIVO**		Bottle	*bot-teel-ya* **BOTTIGLIA**
Beer	*bee-ra* **BIRRA**		Half-bottle	*met-sa bot-teel-ya* **MEZZA BOTTIGLIA**
Bourbon	*berbon* **BOURBON**		Glass	*beekee-yair-ray* **BICCHIERE**
Brandy	*brandy* **BRANDY**		Litre	*lee-tro* **LITRO**
Cider	*see-dro* **SIDRO**			
Claret	*keeyar-ret-toh* **CHIARETTO**		Dry	*sec-ko* **SECCO**
Cocktail	*cocktail* **COCKTAIL**		Full-bodied	*pee-yay-no* **PIENO**
Cognac	*con-yack* **COGNAC**		Light-bodied	*led-jair-ro* **LEGGERO**
Cordial (US)	*lee-kwor-ray* **LIQUORE**		Medium	*met-so* **MEZZO**
Gin (& tonic)	*gin (ay ton-neeko)* **GIN (E TONICO)**		Red	*ross-oh* **ROSSO**
Lager	*bee-ra* **BIRRA**		Rosé	*rozat-tel-lo* **ROSATELLO**
Liqueur	*lee-kwor-ray* **LIQUORE**		Sparking	*spoo-man-tay* **SPUMANTE**
Port	*por-toh* **PORTO**		Sweet	*dol-chay* **DOLCE**
Rum (& coke)	*room (ay coca-cola)* **RUM (E COCA-COLA)**		White	*bee-yang-ko* **BIANCO**
Scotch	*scotch* **SCOTCH**			
Sherry	*sherry* **SHERRY**	some *del* **DEL**		
Vermouth	*vair-moot* **VERMOUTH**	a *oon* **UN**	Double	*dop-peeyo* **DOPPIO**
Vodka	*vodka* **VODKA**	and *ay* **E**	Straight/Neat	*lee-sho* **LISCIO**
Wine	*vee-no* **VINO**	with *con* **CON**	Dry ginger	*zent-sairo dry* **ZENZERO DRY**
Whisky	*whisky* **WHISKY**		with Ice	*con ghee-yat-cho* **CON GHIACCIO**
		1 *oo-no*	Soda	*soda* **SODA**
		2 *doo-ay*	Tonic	*ton-neeka* **TONICA**
		3 *tray*		
		4 *kwat-ro*		
CHEERS!	*cheen-cheen* **CIN-CIN!**	5 *cheen-kway*	Water	*ak-wa* **ACQUA**
		6 *say-ee*		

soft drinks: 31B

? I *ee-yo*
IO

my *eel* **mee**-*yo*
IL MIO

we *noy*
NOI

our *noss*-*tro*
NOSTRO

you *lay*-*ee*
LEI

not *non*
NON

no *non*
NON

would like	*vor-**ray**-ee* **VORREI**	
can I have	*poss-o ah-**vair**-ray* **POSSO AVERE**	
can we have	*possee-**yar**-mo ah-**vair**-ray* **POSSIAMO AVERE**	
is	*eh* **È**	
are	*so-no* **SONO**	
Pay	*pa-**gar**-ray* **PAGARE**	

where *doh-vay*
DOVE

what *koh-sa*
COSA

this *kwess-toh*
QUESTO

now *a-**dess**-o*
ADESSO

later *pee-**yoo** **tar**-dee*
PIÙ TARDI

and *ay*
E

in *dee*
DI

maybe *for-say*
FORSE

of *dee*
DI

with *con*
CON

PAYING *pagga-**men**-toh*
PAGAMENTO

bill/check *con-toh*
CONTO

together *eensee-**yay**-may*
INSIEME

separately *sepparratta-**men**-tay*
SEPARATAMENTE

service *sairveet-**see**-yo*
SERVIZIO

taxes *tass-ah*
TASSA

included *com-press-oh*
COMPRESO

credit card *car-ta cred-eeto*
CARTA CREDITO

mistake *air-**ror**-ray*
ERRORE

small change *ress-toh*
RESTO

HOW MUCH IS (THAT)? *kwan-toh coss-ta*
QUANTO COSTA?

WHAT IS THIS FOR? *ah kay **sair**-vay*
A CHE SERVE?

THAT WAS VERY GOOD! *air-rah mol-toh bwoh-no*
ERA MOLTO BUONO!

SNACKS *spoon-**tee**-nee*
SPUNTINI

Biscuits (UK) *beess-**kot**-tee*
BISCOTTI

Bread *par-nay*
PANE

Butter *boo-ro*
BURRO

Cake *tor-ta*
TORTA

Candy (US) *dol-**choo**-mee*
DOLCIUMI

(bar of) *(stec-ka dee)*
(STECCA DI)

Chocolate *choco-**lar**-ta*
CIOCCOLATA

Cookies (US) *beess-**kot**-tee*
BISCOTTI

Hamburger *am-**boo**-gair*
HAMBURGER

Hot-dog *ott-dog*
HOT-DOG

Ice-cream *jel-**lar**-toh*
GELATO

Open sandwich *trammet-**see**-no*
TRAMEZZINO

Pastry *dol-chee*
DOLCI

Pie *pas-**tee**-cho*
PASTICCIO

Pizza slice *peet-**set**-ta*
PIZZETTA

Roll *pa-**nee**-no*
PANINO

Salad *eensal-**lar**-ta*
INSALATA

Sandwich *sandwich*
SANDWICH

Sweets (UK) *dol-**choo**-mee*
DOLCIUMI

Toast *toast*
TOAST

Toasted sandwich *pan-**nee**-no toss-**tar**-toh*
PANINO TOSTATO

Waffle *chal-day*
CIALDE

soft drinks: 31B   money & tipping: 50A

?	I	*ee-yo* **IO**
	you	*lay-ee* **LEI**
	not	*non* **NON**
	no	*non* **NON**
	which	*kwar-lay* **QUALE**
	where	*doh-vay* **DOVE**
	when	*kwan-doh* **QUANDO**
	what	*koh-sa* **COSA**
	what time	*kay or-ra* **CHE ORA**
	how many	*kwan-tee* **QUANTI**
	how much	*kwan-toh* **QUANTO**
	near	*vee-chee-no* **VICINO**
	here	*kwee* **QUI**
	there	*lar* **LÀ**
	this	*kwess-toh* **QUESTO**
	that	*kwel-loh* **QUELLO**
	these	*kwess-tee* **QUESTI**
	those	*kwel-lee* **QUELLI**

would like	*vor-ray-ee* **VORREI**	can I	*poss-o* **POSSO**
want	*vwar-lay* **VUOLE**	can I have	*poss-o ah-vair-ray* **POSSO AVERE**
have	*oh* **HO**	can you	*pwoh* **PUÒ**
have	*ah* **HA**	Buy	*com-prar-ray* **COMPRARE**
do you have	*ah-vet-tay* **AVETE**	Cut	*tal-yar-ray* **TAGLIARE**
is	*eh* **È**	Pay	*pa-gar-ray* **PAGARE**
are	*so-no* **SONO**	Show me	*mee moss-tree* **MI MOSTRI**
is there	*chay* **C'È**	See	*ved-dair-ray* **VEDERE**
		Wrap	*eencar-tar-ray* **INCARTARE**
		Write down	*scree-vair-ray* **SCRIVERE**

per	*al* **AL**	open	*a-pair-toh* **APERTO**
each	*loo-no* **L'UNO**	closed	*kee-oo-zo* **CHIUSO**
receipt	*reechay-voo-ta* **RICEVUTA**		
bag	*bor-sa* **BORSA**	food	*chee-bo* **CIBO**
carrier bag	*sac-ket-toh* **SACCHETTO**	drinks	*bee-beetay* **BIBITE**

HOW MUCH IS/ARE *kwan-toh eh* **QUANTO È?**

THAT'S FINE *va bay-nay* **VA BENE**

HOW MUCH IS ALL THAT? *kwan-toh vee-yay-nay eel too-toh* **QUANTO VIENE IL TUTTO?**

a	and	any	from	of	off	some
oon **UN**	*ay* **E**	*kwal-kay* **QUALCHE**	*dah* **DA**	*dee* **DI**	*dee* **DI**	*del* **DEL**

fruits & meats: 34A   fish: 34B   groceries: 35A   vegetables & herbs: 35B

100gm	oo-**net**-toh	a little	oon poh **UN PÒ**
125gm	oo-**net**-toh ay oon kwar-toh	more	pee-**yoo** **PIÙ**
250gm	**doo**-way et-tee ay met-so	less	**may**-no **MENO**
½	**met**-so		
1	**oo**-no		
2	**doo**-way	bigger	pee-**yoo gran**-day **PIÙ GRANDE**
3	tray		
4	**kwat**-ro	smaller	pee-**yoo** pee-ko-lo **PIÙ PICCOLO**
5	**cheen**-kway		
6	**say**-ee	better	meel-**yor**-ray **MIGLIORE**
7	**set**-tay		
8	**ot**-toh	cheaper	**may**-no **car**-ro **MENO CARO**
9	**no**-vay		
10	dee-**yay**-chee		
kilo	**kee**-lo **CHILO**		
litre	**lee**-tro **LITRO**	with	con **CON**
		without	**sent**-sa **SENZA**
a	oon **UN**		
of	dee **DI**	nearest:	pee-**yoo** vee-**chee**-no **PIÙ VICINO**
		Baker	pannetair-**ree**-ya **PANETTERIA**
Bottle	bot-**teel**-ya **BOTTIGLIA**	Butcher	matchellair-**ree**-ya **MACELLERIA**
Box	scar-toh-la **SCATOLA**	Confectioner	pasteechair-**ree**-ya **PASTICCERIA**
Can/Tin	bah-**rat**-toh-lo **BARATTOLO**	Dairy	lartair-**ree**-ya **LATTERIA**
Frozen	soorjel-**lar**-toh **SURGELATO**	Delicatessen	saloomair-**ree**-ya **SALUMERIA**
Jar	var-so **VASO**	Fishmonger	peskair-**ree**-ya **PESCHERIA**
Packet	pac-**ket**-toh **PACCHETTO**	Greengrocer	neg-go-tseeyo dee **froo**-ta ay vair-**doo**-ra **NEGOZIO DI FRUTTA E VERDURA**
Piece	**pet**-so **PEZZO**	Grocer	drogair-**ree**-ya **DROGHERIA**
Slice	**fet**-ta **FETTA**	Market	mair-**car**-toh **MERCATO**
Tube	cop-**pet**-ta **COPPETTA**	Supermarket	soopairmair-**car**-toh **SUPERMERCATO**
		(Wine/liquor) shop	ven-**dee**-ta (vee-nee/lee-**kwor**-ree) **VENDITA (VINI LIQUORI)**

SVENDITA = SALE

alcoholic drinks: 32A   soft drinks: 31B   money: 50A

FRUIT	*froo-ta* **FRUTTA**		MEAT	*car-nay* **CARNE**
Apples	*mel-lay* **MELE**		Bacon	*pan-chet-ta* **PANCETTA**
Apricots	*albee-cok-kay* **ALBICOCCHE**		Beef	*mant-so* **MANZO**
Bananas	*bar-nar-nay* **BANANE**		Chicken	*pol-lo* **POLLO**
Cherries	*cheelee-ay-jay* **CILIEGE**		Ham	*pror-shoo-toh* **PROSCIUTTO**
Figs	*fee-kee* **FICHI**		Game	*selva-jee-na* **SELVAGGINA**
Grapefruit	*pom-pell-mo* **POMPELMO**		Lamb	*an-yel-lo* **AGNELLO**
Grapes	*oo-va* **UVA**		Pork	*my-yar-lay* **MAIALE**
Lemons	*lee-mo-nay* **LIMONE**		Turkey	*tac-kee-no* **TACCHINO**
Limes	*ched-ree* **CEDRI**		Veal	*vee-tel-lo* **VITELLO**
Melon	*mel-lo-nay* **MELONE**			
Nuts	*not-chee* **NOCI**		Bone	*oss-so* **OSSO**
Olives	*ol-lee-vay* **OLIVE**		Chop	*brat-cho-la* **BRACIOLA**
Oranges	*ar-ran-cha* **ARANCIA**		Cutlet	*costo-let-ta* **COSTOLETTA**
Peaches	*pess-kay* **PESCHE**		Fat	*grass-so* **GRASSO**
Pears	*pair-ray* **PERE**		Joint	*rot-tolo dee car-nay* **ROTOLO DI CARNE**
Pineapple	*anna-nass* **ANANAS**		Kidneys	*ron-yo-nee* **ROGNONI**
Plums	*proon-yay* **PRUGNE**		Liver	*feg-gartoh* **FEGATO**
Pomegranates	*mella-grar-nay* **MELAGRANE**		Mince	*car-nay tree-tar-ta* **CARNE TRITATA**
Raisins	*oo-va pass-sa* **UVA PASSA**		Ribs	*coss-toh-la* **COSTOLA**
Raspberries	*lam-po-nee* **LAMPONI**		Sausages	*sal-see-chay* **SALSICCE**
Strawberries	*frar-go-lay* **FRAGOLE**		Steak	*bees-tec-ka* **BISTECCA**
Tangerines	*mandar-ree-nee* **MANDARINI**		Tongue	*leeng-gwa* **LINGUA**

game & poultry: 29A

FISH *pesh-ay* **PESCE**		Pike *loo-cho* **LUCCIO**
Anchovies *at-choo-gay* **ACCIUGHE**		Plaice *passair-ree-no/peeya-noot-sa* **PASSERINO PIANUZZA**
Bass *brant-see-no* **BRANZINO**		Prawns *gam-bair-ree* **GAMBERI**
Carp *car-pa* **CARPA**		Salmon *sal-moh-nay* **SALMONE**
Caviar *carvee-yar-lay* **CAVIALE**		Sardines *sar-dee-nay* **SARDINE**
Clams *vong-go-lay* **VONGOLE**		Scallops *ar-sel-lay* **ARSELLE**
Cod *mair-loot-so* **MERLUZZO**		Scampi *scam-pee* **SCAMPI**
Crab *grang-keeyo* **GRANCHIO**		Shrimps *gambair-ret-tee* **GAMBERETTI**
Crayfish *gam-bairo* **GAMBERO**		Sole *sor-leeyo-la* **SOGLIOLA**
Cuttlefish *sep-peeya* **SEPPIA**		Squid *calla-mar-ree* **CALAMARI**
Eel *ang-gwee-la* **ANGUILLA**		Sturgeon *storee-yo-nay* **STORIONE**
Hake *nah-zel-lo* **NASELLO**		Swordfish *pesh-ay spar-da* **PESCE SPADA**
Halibut *pas-saira* **PASSERA**		Tench *teen-ka* **TINCA**
Herring *ar-reeng-gah* **ARINGA**		Trout *trot-ta* **TROTA**
John Dory *san pee-yet-ro* **SAN PIETRO**		Tuna *ton-no* **TONNO**
Lamprey *lam-pray-day* **LAMPREDE**		Whitebait *beeyang-ket-tee* **BIANCHETTI**
Lobster *arra-goss-ta* **ARAGOSTA**		Whiting *mair-lar-no* **MERLANO**
Mackerel *zgom-bro* **SGOMBRO**		
Mullet *treel-yay* **TRIGLIE**		fillet *fee-let-toh* **FILETTO**
Mussels *coat-say* **COZZE**		fingers *baston-chee-nee dee pesh-ay* **BASTONCINI DI PESCE**
Octopus *pol-po* **POLPO**		fresh *fress-co* **FRESCO**
Oysters *oss-treekay* **OSTRICHE**		frozen *soorjel-lar-toh* **SURGELATO**
Perch *pesh-ay pair-seeko* **PESCE PERSICO**		smoked *affoomee-car-toh* **AFFUMICATO**

GROCERIES	*aleemen-tar-ree* **ALIMENTARI**
Baby food	*alee-men-tee pair bam-bee-nee* **ALIMENTI PER BAMBINI**
Beer	*bee-ra* **BIRRA**
Biscuits (UK)	*bees-cot-tee* **BISCOTTI**
Bread	*par-nay* (rolls) *(par-nee-nee)* **PANE** **(PANINI)**
Butter	*boo-ro* **BURRO**
Cake	*dol-chay/tor-ta* **DOLCE TORTA**
Candy (US)	*dol-choo-mee* **DOLCIUMI**
Cereal	*fee-yoc-kee dar-ven-nah* **FIOCCHI D'AVENA**
Chocolate	*choco-lar-ta* **CIOCCOLATA**
Cheese	*for-mar-jo* **FORMAGGIO**
Coffee	*caf-fay* **CAFFÈ**
Cold cuts	*affet-tar-tee* **AFFETTATI**
Cookies (US)	*beess-cot-tee* **BISCOTTI**
Cooking oil/fat	*grar-see/ol-yo* **GRASSI OLIO**
Cream	*par-na* **PANNA**
Dried herbs	*air-bay sec-kay* **ERBE SECCHE**
Eggs	*woh-va* **UOVA**
Flour	*far-ree-na* **FARINA**
Fruit juice	*soo-ko dee froo-ta* **SUCCO DI FRUTTA**
Hamburgers	*am-boo-gair* **HAMBURGER**
Honey	*mee-yel-lay* **MIELE**
Ice cream	*jel-lar-toh* **GELATO**
Jam	*marmel-lar-ta* **MARMELLATA**
Margarine	*margga-ree-na* **MARGARINA**
Marmalade	*marmel-lar-ta* **MARMELLATA**
Milk	*lar-tay* **LATTE**
Mustard	*sen-narpay* **SENAPE**
Olive oil	*ol-yo dee ol-lee-va* **OLIO DI OLIVA**
Pickles	*sotta-chet-tee* **SOTTACETI**
Pie	*pas-tee-cheeyo* **PASTICCIO**
Rice	*ree-so* **RISO**
Potato chips/crisps	*patta-tee-nas* **PATATINAS**
Salami	*sal-lar-may* **SALAME**
Salt & pepper	*sar-lay ay pay-pay* **SALE E PEPE**
Sandwiches	*sandwich* **SANDWICH**
Spaghetti	*spa-ghet-tee* **SPAGHETTI**
Soft drinks	*bee-beetay* **BIBITE**
Soup	*mee-nes-tra* **MINESTRA**
Sugar	*tsoo-kairo* **ZUCCHERO**
Sweets (UK)	*dol-choo-mee* **DOLCIUMI**
Tea	*tay* **TÈ**
Vinegar	*at-chet-toh* **ACETO**
Wine	*vee-no* **VINO**
Yoghurt	*ee-yor-oort* **YOGURT**

types of cheese: 31A   soft drink flavours (fruits): 34A   chemist/pharmacy: 45

VEGETABLES	*vair-**doo**-ra* **VERDURA**	Peas	*pee-**sel**-lee* **PISELLI**
Artichokes	*car-**chof**-fee* **CARCIOFI**	Peppers/Pimentoes	*peppair-**ro**-nee* **PEPERONI**
Asparagus	*ass-**par**-rargo* **ASPARAGO**	Potatoes	*pat-**tat**-tay* **PATATE**
Aubergines	*melant-**sar**-nay* **MELANZANE**	Pumpkin	*tsoo-ka* **ZUCCA**
Avocado	*avo-**car**-doh* **AVOCADO**	Radishes	*rava-**nel**-lee* **RAVANELLI**
Beetroot	*barbarbee-**yet**-tollay* **BARBABIETOLE**	Shallots	*scal-**lon**-yo* **SCALOGNO**
Broad beans	*far-vay* **FAVE**	Spinach	*spee-**nar**-chee* **SPINACI**
Cabbage	*car-volee* **CAVOLI**	Brusselles Sprouts	*cavvo-lee-nee dee broo-**sail*** **CAVOLINI DI BRUXELLES**
Carrots	*car-rot-tay* **CAROTE**	Sweetcorn	***mah**-ees **dol**-chay* **MAIS DOLCE**
Cauliflower	*cavvolfee-**yor**-ray* **CAVOLFIORE**	Tomatoes	*pommee-**dor**-ro* **POMIDORO**
Celery	***sed**-darno* **SEDANO**	Turnips	***rar**-pay* **RAPE**
Courgettes	*tsoo-**kee**-nee* **ZUCCHINI**	Truffles	*tar-**too**-fee* **TARTUFI**
Cucumber	*chetree-yo-lo* **CETRIOLO**	Zucchini	*tsoo-**kee**-nee* **ZUCCHINI**
Gherkins	*chetreeyo-**lee**-nee* **CETRIOLINI**		
Green beans	*fadjo-**lee**-nee* **FAGIOLINI**	HERBS	***air**-bay* **ERBE**
Leeks	*por-ree* **PORRI**	Basil	*baz-**zee**-leeko* **BASILICO**
Lentils	*len-**tee**-keeyay* **LENTICCHIE**	Bay leaves	*al-**lor**-ro* **ALLORO**
Lettuce	*lattoo-ga* **LATTUGA**	Garlic	***al**-yo* **AGLIO**
Marrow	*tsoo-ka* **ZUCCA**	Mint	***men**-ta* **MENTA**
Mushrooms	***foong**-ghee* **FUNGHI**	Rosemary	*rozmar-**ree**-no* **ROSMARINO**
Onions	*chee-**po**-lay* **CIPOLLE**	Sage	***sal**-veeya* **SALVIA**
Parsley	*pret-**sem**-mo-lo* **PREZZEMOLO**	Tarragon	*drargon-**chel**-lo* **DRAGONCELLO**
Parsnip	*pastee-**nac**-ka* **PASTINACA**	Thyme	***teemo*** **TIMO**

?	I	*ee-yo* **IO**	would like	*vor-ray-ee* **VORREI**	can I	*poss-o* **POSSO**
	me	*may* **ME**	want	*vwar-lay* **VUOLE**	can I have	*poss-o ahvair-ay* **POSSO AVERE**
	my	*eel mee-yo* **IL MIO**				
	you	*lay-ee* **LEI**	have	*oh* **HO**	Alter	*cambeeyar-ray* **CAMBIARE**
			have	*ah* **HA**	Help me	*mee ah-ee-yoo-tee* **MI AIUTI**
	not	*non* **NON**	do you have	*ah-vet-tay* **AVETE**	Like	*peeya-chair-ray* **PIACERE**
	no	*non* **NON**			Measure	*meezoo-rar-ray* **MISURARE**
			is	*eh* **È**	Pay	*pa-gar-ray* **PAGARE**
	which	*kwar-lay* **QUALE**	are	*so-no* **SONO**	will be Ready	*sar-rah pron-toh* **SARÀ PRONTO**
	where	*doh-vay* **DOVE**	is there	*chay* **C'È**	See	*ved-dair-ray* **VEDERE**
	when	*kwan-doh* **QUANDO**			Send	*sped-dee-ray* **SPEDIRE**
	what	*koh-sa* **COSA**	can you	*pwoh* **PUÒ**	Try on	*pro-var-ray* **PROVARE**

			each	*loo-no* **L'UNO**	nearest	*pee-yoo vee-chee-no* **PIÙ VICINO**
what time	*kay or-ra* **CHE ORA**		per metre	*al met-ro* **AL METRO**	name	*no-may* **NOME**
					address	*eendee-reet-so* **INDIRIZZO**
how many	*kwan-tee* **QUANTI**					
how much	*kwan-toh* **QUANTO**		receipt	*reechay-voo-ta* **RICEVUTA**	open	*a-pair-toh* **APERTO**
			refund	*reem-bor-so* **RIMBORSO**	closed	*kee-oo-zo* **CHIUSO**
near	*vee-chee-no* **VICINO**					
here	*kwee* **QUI**			THAT'S FINE	*va bay-nay* **VA BENE**	
there	*lar* **LÀ**			HOW MUCH IS (THAT)?	*kwan-toh coss-ta* **QUANTO COSTA?**	
this	*kwess-toh* **QUESTO**					

			and	at	for	from	in	on	to
these	*kwess-tee* **QUESTI**		*ay* **E**	*al* **AL**	*pair* **PER**	*dah* **DA**	*een* **IN**	*soo* **SU**	*ah* **A**

---

money: 50A   time: 60   types of clothes: 37

something	*kwal-co-sa* **QUALCOSA**		colour	*col-lor-ray* **COLORE**	size	*mee-zoo-ra* **MISURA**
good	*bwoh-no* **BUONO**		shape	*for-ma* **FORMA**	style	*stee-lay* **STILE**
inexpensive	*eco-nom-meeco* **ECONOMICO**					
simple	*sem-pleechay* **SEMPLICE**		material	*stof-fa* **STOFFA**		
similar	*see-meelay* **SIMILE**		pattern	*fanta-zee-ya* **FANTASIA**	plain	*teen-ta oo-neeta* **TINTA UNITA**
same	*low stess-so* **LO STESSO**		spots	*pal-lee-nee* **PALLINI**	stripes	*ree-gay* **RIGHE**
different	*dee-vair-so* **DIVERSO**		check	*kwad-ree* **QUADRI**		
matching	*kay see accom-parn-ya* **CHE SI ACCOMPAGNA**					
too	*trop-po* **TROPPO**		imported	*eempor-tar-toh* **IMPORTATO**		
more	*pee-yoo* **PIÙ**		hand-made	*fat-toh ah mar-no* **FATTO A MANO**		
less	*may-no* **MENO**		made in Italy	*fabree-car-toh een ee-tal-yah* **FABBRICATO IN ITALIA**		
medium	*med-deeyo* **MEDIO**		display case	*scarf-far-lay* **SCAFFALE**		
large	*gran-day* **GRANDE**	small *pee-ko-lo* **PICCOLO**	fitting room	*ca-bee-na dee pro-va* **CABINA DI PROVA**		
wide	*lar-gay* **LARGHE**	narrow *stret-tay* **STRETTE**	mirror	*spec-keeyo* **SPECCHIO**		
long	*loong-go* **LUNGO**	short *cor-toh* **CORTO**	shop window	*vet-tree-na* **VETRINA**		
light	*kee-yar-ro* **CHIARO**	dark *scoo-ro* **SCURO**	nearest	*pee-yoo vee-chee-no* **PIÙ VICINO**		
light	*led-jair-ro* **LEGGERO**	heavy *pess-san-tay* **PESANTE**	Dept store	*gran-day maggat-see-no* **GRANDE MAGAZZINO**		
thick	*spess-so* **SPESSO**	thin *fee-nay* **FINE**	Dress shop	*confetsee-yo-nay pair seen-yor-ra* **CONFEZIONI PER SIGNORA**		
loose	*lar-go* **LARGO**	tight *stret-toh* **STRETTO**	Menswear	*confetsee-yo-nee pair woh-mo* **CONFEZIONI PER UOMO**		
top	*al-toh* **ALTO**	bottom *fon-doh* **FONDO**	Shoe shop	*neg-go-tseeyo dee scar-pay* **NEGOZIO DI SCARPE**		
middle	*met-so* **MEZZO**	side *lar-toh* **LATO**	Sports shop	*bot-tay-ga pair lo sport* **BOTTEGA PER LO SPORT**		

SVENDITA = SALE

---

materials & colours: 38A   sizes: 38B   jewelry: 42   cosmetics: 46B

for men	*pair woh-mo* **PER UOMO**	Dressing gown	*vess-tay dah cam-mairra* **VESTE DA CAMERA**
for women	*pair don-na* **PER DONNA**	Evening dress	*ar-beetoh dah sair-ra* **ABITO DA SERA**
for boy	*pair rag-gat-see* **PER RAGAZZI**	Flip flops	*corray-yar-nay* **COREANE**
for girl	*pair rag-gat-say* **PER RAGAZZE**	Frock	*ar-beetoh* **ABITO**
for baby	*pair bam-bee-no* **PER BAMBINO**	Girdle	*boos-toh* **BUSTO**
		Gloves	*gwan-tee* **GUANTI**
CLOTHES	*ves-tee-tee* **VESTITI**	Handbag	*bor-sa* **BORSA**
Anorak	*jac-ka ah ven-toh* **GIACCA A VENTO**	Handkerchief	*fattsol-let-toh* **FAZZOLETTO**
Bath robe	*accapat-toh-eeyo* **ACCAPPATOIO**	Hat	*cap-pel-lo* **CAPPELLO**
Bathing cap	*coo-feeya dah ban-yo* **CUFFIA DA BAGNO**	Jacket	*cass-sar-ka* **CASACCA**
Bikini	*bikini* **BIKINI**	Jeans	*jeans* **JEANS**
Blouse	*bloo-za* **BLUSA**	Jersey	*camee-chet-ta ah marl-ya* **CAMICETTA A MAGLIA**
Boots	*stee-var-lee* **STIVALI**	Negligé	*neglee-jay* **NEGLIGÉ**
Bow tie	*cra-vat-ta ah far-far-la* **CRAVATTA A FARFALLA**	Nightdress	*camee-cha da not-tay* **CAMICIA DA NOTTE**
Bra	*redjee-sen-no* **REGGISENO**	Overalls	*too-ta* **TUTA**
Braces	*bret-tel-lay* **BRETELLE**	Overcoat	*sop-pra-beetoh* **SOPRABITO**
Briefs	*moo-tan-day dah woh-mo* **MUTANDE DA UOMO**	Panties	*caltson-chee-nee dah don-na* **CALZONCINI DA DONNA**
Cap	*bair-ret-toh* **BERRETTO**	Pants (US)	*panta-lo-nee* **PANTALONI**
Cape	*man-tel-lo* **MANTELLO**	Panty girdle	*cor-set-toh* **CORSETTO**
Cardigan	*jac-ka dee lar-na* **GIACCA DI LANA**	Panty hose	*col-lant* **COLLANT**
Coat	*sop-prar-beetoh* **SOPRABITO**	Petticoat	*sottoh-ves-tay* **SOTTOVESTE**
Dinner jacket	*smoking* **SMOKING**	Pullover	*poo-lo-ver* **PULLOVER**
Dress	*ves-tee-toh* **VESTITO**	Purse (US)	*bor-sa* **BORSA**

---

materials & colours: 38A   **sizes: 38B**

Pyjamas	*pee-**jar**-ma*	**PIGIAMA**
Raincoat	*eempairmee-**yar**-beelay*	**IMPERMEABILE**
Sandals	*san-darlee*	**SANDALI**
Scarf	***shar**-pa*	**SCIARPA**
Shirt	*cam-**mee**-cha*	**CAMICIA**
Shoes	*scar-pay*	**SCARPE**
Shorts	*pantalon-**chee**-nee*	**PANTALONCINI**
Skirt	*gon-na*	**GONNA**
Slip	*sottoh-**vess**-tay*	**SOTTOVESTE**
Slippers	*pan-**toh**-follay*	**PANTOFOLE**
Socks	***calt**-say*	**CALZE**
Sports jacket	*jac-ka spor-**tee**-va*	**GIACCA SPORTIVA**
Stockings	***calt**-say*	**CALZE**
Suit (man's)	*vess-**tee**-toh*	**VESTITO**
Suit (woman's)	*tie-**yer***	**TAILLEUR**
Suspenders (US)	*bret-**tel**-lay*	**BRETELLE**
Sweater	*mal-yo-nay*	**MAGLIONE**
Sweatshirt	*mal-**yet**-ta*	**MAGLIETTA**
Swimsuit	*coss-**too**-may dah **ban**-yo*	**COSTUME DA BAGNO**
Swimming trunks	*caltson-**chee**-nee dah **ban**-yo*	**CALZONCINI DA BAGNO**
Tennis shoes	*scar-pay dah tennis*	**SCARPE DA TENNIS**
Tie	*crav-**vat**-ta*	**CRAVATTA**
Tights	*col-**lant***	**COLLANT**

Towel	*ashooga-**mar**-no*	**ASCIUGAMANO**
Track suit	***too**-ta dah **cor**-sa*	**TUTA DA CORSA**
Trousers (UK)	*panta-**lo**-nee*	**PANTALONI**
T shirt	*cannotee-**yair**-ra*	**CANOTTIERA**
Undershirt (US)	*cammee-**cho**-la*	**CAMICIOLA**
Underpants (UK)	*moo-**tan**-day dah **woh**-mo*	**MUTANDE DA UOMO**
Vest (UK)	*cammee-**cho**-la*	**CAMICIOLA**
with:	*con*	**CON:**
<u>ACCESSORIES</u>	*atchess-**sor**-ree*	<u>**ACCESSORI**</u>
Belt	*cheen-**too**-ra*	**CINTURA**
Buckle	*fee-beeya*	**FIBBIA**
Button	*bot-**toh**-nay*	**BOTTONE**
Cuffs	*pol-**see**-nee*	**POLSINI**
Elastic	*el-**las**-teeko*	**ELASTICO**
Pocket	*tass-ka*	**TASCA**
Pocket book (US)	*borsel-**lee**-no*	**BORSELLINO**
Purse (UK)	*borsel-**lee**-no*	**BORSELLINO**
Shoe laces	*lat-chee dah scar-pay*	**LACCI DA SCARPE**
Shoe polish	*loo-cheedoh*	**LUCIDO**
Umbrella	*om-**brel**-lo*	**OMBRELLO**
Wallet	*porta-**foll**-yo*	**PORTAFOGLIO**
Zip	*lam-po*	**LAMPO**

jewelry: 42   cosmetics: 46B

MATERIALS	*stof-fa* **STOFFA**	Terylene	*tair-reetal* **TERITAL**
Chiffon	*shee-fon* **CHIFFON**	Tweed	*tweed* **TWEED**
Corduroy	*vel-loo-toh ah coss-tay* **VELLUTO A COSTE**	Velvet	*vel-loo-toh* **VELLUTO**
Cotton	*cot-toh-nay* **COTONE**	Wool	*lar-na* **LANA**
Crepe	*cress-po* **CRESPO**	Worsted	*pettee-nar-toh* **PETTINATO**
Denim	*tel-la pair blue-jeans* **TELA PER BLUE-JEANS**	dryclean only	*poo-lee-ray solo ah sec-ko* **PULIRE SOLO A SECCO**
Felt	*fel-tro* **FELTRO**	hand wash only	*la-var-ray solo ah mar-no* **LAVARE SOLO A MANO**
Flannel	*flan-nel-la* **FLANELLA**	non-iron	*non stee-rar-ray* **NON STIRARE**
Fur	*pel-lee-cha* **PELLICCIA**		
(artificial)	*(arteefee-char-lay)* **(ARTIFICIALE)**		
Gabardine	*gabar-deen* **GABARDINE**	COLOURS	*col-lor-ray* **COLORE**
Lace	*peet-so* **PIZZO**	too	*trop-po* **TROPPO**
Leather	*pel-lay* **PELLE**	more	*pee-yoo* **PIÙ**
Linen	*lee-no* **LINO**		
Nylon	*nye-lon* **NYLON**	Beige	*beige* **BEIGE**
Polyester	*pollee-ess-tair-ray* **POLIESTERE**	Black	*nair-ro* **NERO**
Poplin	*popair-leen* **POPELINE**	Blue	*bloo* **BLU**
Rayon	*rah-eeyon* **RAION**	Brown	*mar-roh-nay* **MARRONE**
Rubber	*gom-ma* **GOMMA**	Cream	*cray-ma* **CREMA**
Satin	*rar-so* **RASO**	Crimson	*crem-meezee* **CREMISI**
Silk	*set-ta* **SETA**	Fawn	*fool-vo* **FULVO**
Serge	*sye-ya* **SAIA**	Emerald	*smair-ral-doh* **SMERALDO**
Suede	*pel-lay scammo-shat-ta* **PELLE SCAMOSCIATA**	Gold	*or-ro* **ORO**
		Green	*vair-day* **VERDE**

Colours (second column):

bright	*vee-var-chee* **VIVACI**
dull	*scoo-ree* **SCURI**
Grey	*gree-jo* **GRIGIO**
Mauve	*mal-va* **MALVA**
Orange	*arran-cho-nay* **ARANCIONE**
Pink	*ro-za* **ROSA**
Purple	*vee-yo-la* **VIOLA**
Red	*ross-so* **ROSSO**
Silver	*ar-jen-toh* **ARGENTO**
Tan	*ros-see-cho* **ROSSICCIO**
White	*bee-yang-ko* **BIANCO**
Yellow	*jal-low* **GIALLO**

SIZES

Because UK, US and Continental sizes do not all exactly coincide, these sizes are only near equivalents:

LADIES DRESSES/SUITS TROUSERS/JACKETS

UK	10	12	14	16	18	20	22
	30	32	34	36	38	40	42
US	8	10	12	14	16	18	20
CONTINENTAL	36	38	40	42	44	46	48

LADIES SWEATERS

UK/US	32	34	36	38	40	42
CONTINENTAL	36	38	40	42	44	46

LADIES STOCKINGS

UK/US	8	$8\frac{1}{2}$	9	$9\frac{1}{2}$	10	$10\frac{1}{2}$
CONTINENTAL	0	1	2	3	4	5

LADIES & MENS HATS

UK	$6\frac{5}{8}$	$6\frac{3}{4}$	$6\frac{7}{8}$	7	$7\frac{1}{8}$	$7\frac{1}{4}$	$7\frac{3}{8}$	$7\frac{1}{2}$	$7\frac{5}{8}$
US	$6\frac{3}{4}$	$6\frac{7}{8}$	7	$7\frac{1}{8}$	$7\frac{1}{4}$	$7\frac{3}{8}$	$7\frac{1}{2}$	$7\frac{5}{8}$	$7\frac{3}{4}$
CONTINENTAL	54	55	56	57	58	59	60	61	62

LADIES & MENS SHOES

UK	3	$3\frac{1}{2}$	4	$4\frac{1}{2}$	5	$5\frac{1}{2}$	6	$6\frac{1}{2}$	7	$7\frac{1}{2}$
US	$4\frac{1}{2}$	5	$5\frac{1}{2}$	6	$6\frac{1}{2}$	7	$7\frac{1}{2}$	8	$8\frac{1}{2}$	9
CONTINENTAL	35	36	37	$37\frac{1}{2}$	38	$38\frac{1}{2}$	39	$39\frac{1}{2}$	40	$40\frac{1}{2}$

MENS SUITS

UK/US	36	38	40	42	44	46
CONTINENTAL	46	48	50	52	54	56

MENS SHIRTS

UK/US	14	$14\frac{1}{2}$	15	$15\frac{1}{2}$	16	$16\frac{1}{2}$	17
CONTINENTAL	36	37	38	39	41	42	43

WAIST, CHEST & BUST MEASUREMENTS

inches	24	26	28	30	32	34	36
CENTIMETRES	61	66	71	76	81	86	91
inches	38	40	42	44	46	48	50
CENTIMETRES	97	102	107	112	117	122	127

?	I	*ee-yo* **IO**
	you	*lay-ee* **LEI**
	not	*non* **NON**
	no	*non* **NON**
	which	*kwar-lay* **QUALE**
	where	*doh-vay* **DOVE**
	when	*kwan-doh* **QUANDO**
	what	*koh-sa* **COSA**

would like	*vor-ray-ee* **VORREI**	can I	*poss-o* **POSSO**
want	*vwarlay* **VUOLE**	can I have	*poss-o ah-vair-ray* **POSSO AVERE**
have	*oh* **HO**	can you	*pwoh* **PUÒ**
have	*ah* **HA**	Get	*pren-dair-ray* **PRENDERE**
do you have	*ah-vet-tay* **AVETE**	Pay	*pa-gar-ray* **PAGARE**
is	*eh* **È**	See	*ved-dair-ray* **VEDERE**
are	*so-no* **SONO**	Show me	*mee moss-tree* **MI MOSTRI**
		Wrap	*eencar-tar-ray* **INCARTARE**

how many	*kwan-tee* **QUANTI**	nearest	*pee-yoo vee-chee-no* **PIÙ VICINO**	good	*bwoh-no* **BUONO**
		open	*a-pair-toh* **APERTO**	cheap	*eco-nom-meeco* **ECONOMICO**
near	*vee-chee-no* **VICINO**	closed	*kee-oo-zo* **CHIUSO**	cheaper	*may-no car-ro* **MENO CARO**
here	*kwee* **QUI**	each	*loo-no* **L'UNO**	better	*meel-yor-ray* **MIGLIORE**
there	*lar* **LÀ**	receipt	*reechay-voo-ta* **RICEVUTA**	bigger	*pee-yoo gran-day* **PIÙ GRANDE**
this	*kwess-toh* **QUESTO**			smaller	*pee-yoo pee-ko-lo* **PIÙ PICCOLO**
these	*kwess-tee* **QUESTI**	bag	*bor-sa* **BORSA**	alternative	*altairna-tee-va* **ALTERNATIVA**

		name	*no-may* **NOME**
THAT'S FINE	*va bay-nay* **VA BENE**	author	*out-tor-ray* **AUTORE**
HOW MUCH IS (THAT)?	*kwan-toh coss-ta* **QUANTO COSTA?**	publisher	*edee-tor-ray* **EDITORE**
		local	*loc-kar-lay* **LOCALE**

at	by	for	in	of	about		Italian	*eetal-yar-no* **ITALIANO**
al **AL**	*dee* **DI**	*pair* **PER**	*dee* **DI**	*dee* **DI**	*ser-ka* **CIRCA**			

stationery & art supplies: 40   **money: 50A**

<u>BOOKSHOP</u>	*leebrair-reeya* **LIBRERIA**	<u>TOBACCONIST</u>	*ta-bac-kee* **TABACCHI**
<u>NEWSAGENT</u>	*jornar-lar-reeyo* **GIORNALAIO**	Battery	*pee-la* **PILA**
<u>NEWSTAND</u>	*kee-yosko* **CHIOSCO**	Cigar	*see-garro* **SIGARO**
Atlas	*at-lan-tay* **ATLANTE**	box of Cigars	*ska-toh-la dee see-garree* **SCATOLA DI SIGARI**
Book	*lee-bro* **LIBRO**	Cigarettes	*seegar-ret-tay* **SIGARETTE**
Dictionary	*deetseeyo-nar-reeyo* **DIZIONARIO**	packet/carton	*pac-ket-tee/ stec-ka* **PACCHETTI STECCA**
Guide book	*gwee-da* **GUIDA**	filter	*feel-tro* **FILTRO**
Magazine	*ree-veess-ta* **RIVISTA**	king-size	*for-mar-toh gran-day* **FORMATO GRANDE**
Map	*car-ta jayo-graf-feeka* **CARTA GEOGRAFICA**	english	*eeng-glay-zay* **INGLESE**
(bus/metro)	*(outo-boos/met-ro)* **(AUTOBUS METRO)**	american	*amairree-car-no* **AMERICANO**
(road map)	*(car-ta strar-dar-lay)* **(CARTA STRADALE)**	Flints	*peeyet-tree-nay* **PIETRINE**
(town map)	*(pee-yan-ta della chee-ta)* **(PIANTA DELLA CITTÀ)**	Lighter	*atchen-dee-no* **ACCENDINO**
Newspaper	*jor-nar-lay* **GIORNALE**	(fluid/gas)	*(ben-zee-na/gaz)* **(BENZINA GAZ)**
Paperback	*lee-bro tass-car-beelay* **LIBRO TASCABILE**	box of Matches	*ska-toh-la de feeya-mee-fairree* **SCATOLA DI FIAMMIFERI**
Poster	*por-ster* **POSTER**	Pipe cleaners	*netta-pee-pay* **NETTAPIPE**
Postcard	*carto-lee-nay* **CARTOLINE**	Tobacco	*ta-bac-co* **TABACCO**
Souvenir	*souvenir* **SOUVENIR**	Wick	*stop-pee-no* **STOPPINO**
Travel guide	*gwee-da dee vee-yar-jo* **GUIDA DI VIAGGIO**		
Biography	*beeyo-gra-fee-ya* **BIOGRAFIA**		
Children's	*pair bam-bee-nee* **PER BAMBINI**	strong	*for-tay* **FORTE**
English language	*leeng-gwa eeng-glay-zay* **LINGUA INGLESE**	mild	*med-deeyo* **MEDIO**
Novel	*romant-so* **ROMANZO**	menthol	*men-toh-lo* **MENTOLO**

further subjects: 22B   **sports: 21**   **local places: 18A**   **places in Italy: 24B**

?

| I | *ee-yo* **IO** |
| you | *lay-ee* **LEI** |

| not | *non* **NON** |
| no | *non* **NON** |

which	*kwar-lay* **QUALE**
where	*doh-vay* **DOVE**
when	*kwan-doh* **QUANDO**
what	*koh-sa* **COSA**

would like	*vor-ray-ee* **VORREI**	is there	*chay* **C'È**
want	*vwar-lay* **VUOLE**	can I	*poss-o* **POSSO**
have	*oh* **HO**	can I have	*poss-o ah-vair-ray* **POSSO AVERE**
have	*ah* **HA**	can you	*pwoh* **PUÒ**
do you have	*ah-vet-tay* **AVETE**	Get	*pren-dair-ray* **PRENDERE**
		Pay	*pa-gar-ray* **PAGARE**
is	*eh* **È**	See	*ved-dair-ray* **VEDERE**
are	*so-no* **SONO**	Wrap	*eencar-tar-ray* **INCARTARE**

how many	*kwan-tee* **QUANTI**
near	*vee-chee-no* **VICINO**
here	*kwee* **QUI**
there	*lar* **LÀ**
this	*kwess-toh* **QUESTO**
these	*kwess-tee* **QUESTI**

nearest	*pee-yoo vee-chee-no* **PIÙ VICINO**
open	*a-pair-toh* **APERTO**
closed	*kee-oo-zo* **CHIUSO**
each	*loo-no* **L'UNO**
receipt	*reechay-voo-ta* **RICEVUTA**
bag	*bor-sa* **BORSA**

good	*bwoh-no* **BUONO**
cheap	*eco-nom-meeco* **ECONOMICO**
cheaper	*may-no car-ro* **MENO CARO**
better	*meel-yor-ray* **MIGLIORE**
bigger	*pee-yoo gran-day* **PIÙ GRANDE**
smaller	*pee-yoo pee-ko-lo* **PIÙ PICCOLO**
alternative	*altairna-tee-va* **ALTERNATIVA**
similar	*see-meelay* **SIMILE**
thicker	*pee-yoo spess-so* **PIÙ SPESSO**
thinner	*pee-yoo sot-tee-lay* **PIÙ SOTTILE**
wider	*pee-yoo lar-go* **PIÙ LARGO**
narrower	*pee-yoo stret-toh* **PIÙ STRETTO**

| THAT'S FINE | *va bay-nay* **VA BENE** |
| HOW MUCH IS (THAT)? | *kwan-toh coss-ta* **QUANTO COSTA?** |

at	by	for	in	of	to
al	*dee*	*pair*	*dee*	*dee*	*ah*
AL	**DI**	**PER**	**DI**	**DI**	**A**

money: 50A

STATIONERY	*cartolair-**ree**-ya* **CARTOLERIA**	Tissue paper	*car-ta vel-**lee**-na* **CARTA VELINA**
Ball point pen	*bee-ro* **BIRO**	Typewriter	***mak**-keena da **scree**-vairay* **MACCHINA DA SCRIVERE**
Carbon paper	*car-ta car-**boh**-nay* **CARTA CARBONE**	(paper)	*(**car**-ta)* **(CARTA)**
Cellophane tape	*scotch* **SCOTCH**	(ribbon)	*(**nass**-tro)* **(NASTRO)**
Chalks	*jess-**set**-tee* **GESSETTI**	Wrapping paper	*car-ta dah **pac**-kee* **CARTA DA PACCHI**
Drawings pins	*poon-**tee**-nay dah dee-**sen**-yo* **PUNTINE DA DISEGNO**		
Envelopes	***booss**-tay* **BUSTE**	ART SUPPLIES	*reefornee-**men**-tee **dar**-tay* **RIFORNIMENTI D'ARTE**
Eraser	*gom-ma* **GOMMA**	Acrylic paints	*col-**lor**-ree ac-**ree**-leekee* **COLORI ACRILICI**
File	*car-**tel**-la* **CARTELLA**	Canvas	*tel-la* **TELA**
Fountain pen	***pen**-na steelo-**gra**-feecka* **PENNA STILOGRAFICA**	Charcoal	*carbon-**nel**-la* **CARBONELLA**
Felt-tip pen	*penar-**rel**-lo* **PENNARELLO**	Coloured paper	*car-ta collor-**rar**-ta* **CARTA COLORATA**
Glue	*col-la* **COLLA**	Coloured pencils	*mat-**tee**-tay collor-**rar**-tay* **MATITE COLORATE**
bottle of Ink	*bot-**teel**-ya dee eeng-**kee**-ostro* **BOTTIGLIA DI INCHIOSTRO**	Crayons	*pas-**tel**-lee* **PASTELLI**
Labels	*ettee-**ket**-tay* **ETICHETTE**	Drawing paper	*car-tay dah dee-**sen**-yo* **CARTE DA DISEGNO**
Notebook	*tackoo-**wee**-no* **TACCUINO**	Easel	*cavval-**let**-toh* **CAVALLETTO**
Note paper	*car-ta dah **let**-tair-ray* **CARTA DA LETTERE**	Fixative	*feesat-**tee**-vo* **FISSATIVO**
Pencil	*mat-**tee**-ta* **MATITA**	Oil	*ol-yo* **OLIO**
Pencil sharpener	*tempair-**ree**-no* **TEMPERINO**	Oil paints	*col-**lor**-ree ah **ol**-yo* **COLORI A OLIO**
Playing cards	*car-tay dah **joc**-ko* **CARTE DA GIOCO**	Paint box	*scat-toh-la day col-**lor**-ree* **SCATOLA DEI COLORI**
Refill for:	*ree-**cam**-beeyo pair:* **RICAMBIO PER:**	Paint brush	*pen-**nel**-lo* **PENNELLO**
Rubber	*gom-ma* **GOMMA**	Pastels	*pas-**tel**-lee* **PASTELLI**
Ruler	*ree-ga* **RIGA**	Turpentine	*tremen-**tee**-na* **TREMENTINA**
String	*spar-go* **SPAGO**	Water colours	*akwa-**rel**-lee* **ACQUARELLI**

minerals: 42B   textiles: 38A   colours: 38A

?

I	*ee-yo* **IO**
my	*eel mee-yo* **IL MIO**
you	*lay-ee* **LEI**
not	*non* **NON**
no	*non* **NON**
which	*kwar-lay* **QUALE**
where	*doh-vay* **DOVE**
when	*kwan-doh* **QUANDO**
what	*koh-sa* **COSA**

would like	*vor-ray-ee* **VORREI**	can I	*poss-o* **POSSO**
want	*vwar-lay* **VUOLE**	can I have	*poss-o ah-vair-ray* **POSSO AVERE**
have	*oh* **HO**	can you	*pwoh* **PUÒ**
have	*ah* **HA**	Get	*pren-dair-ray* **PRENDERE**
do you have	*ah-vet-tay* **AVETE**	Pay	*pa-gar-ray* **PAGARE**
is	*eh* **È**	Repair	*reepar-rar-ray* **RIPARARE**
are	*so-no* **SONO**	will be Ready	*sar-rah pron-toh* **SARÀ PRONTO**
is there	*chay* **C'È**	See	*ved-dair-ray* **VEDERE**
		Ship	*sped-dee-ray* **SPEDIRE**

how many	*kwan-tee* **QUANTI**			small	*pee-ko-lo* **PICCOLO**
how old	*kwan-tay an-tee-ko* **QUANT'È ANTICO**	open	*a-pair-toh* **APERTO**	good	*bwoh-no* **BUONO**
		closed	*kee-oo-zo* **CHIUSO**	inexpensive	*eco-nom-meeco* **ECONOMICO**
near	*vee-chee-no* **VICINO**	deposit	*dep-pos-eetoh* **DEPOSITO**		
here	*kwee* **QUI**	receipt	*reechay-voo-ta* **RICEVUTA**	cheaper	*may-no car-ro* **MENO CARO**
this	*kwess-toh* **QUESTO**	name	*no-may* **NOME**	better	*meel-yor-ray* **MIGLIORE**
these	*kwess-tee* **QUESTI**	address	*eendee-reet-so* **INDIRIZZO**	bigger	*pee-yoo gran-day* **PIÙ GRANDE**
				smaller	*pee-yoo pee-ko-lo* **PIÙ PICCOLO**

THAT'S FINE *va bay-nay* **VA BENE**

HOW MUCH IS (THAT)? *kwan-toh coss-ta* **QUANTO COSTA?**

alternative	*altairna-tee-va* **ALTERNATIVA**
simpler	*pee-yoo sem-plee-chay* **PIÙ SEMPLICE**
similar	*see-meelay* **SIMILE**

at	by	for	in	of	to
al	*dee*	*pair*	*dee*	*dee*	*ah*
AL	**DI**	**PER**	**DI**	**DI**	**A**

money: 50A   **textiles: 38A**   **art materials: 40B**

ANTIQUE SHOP	*antee-**kwar**-reeyo* **ANTIQUARIO**	ART GALLERY (SHOP)	*gallair-**ree**-ya **dar**-tay* **GALLERIA D'ARTE**
Boxes	*scat-toh-lay* **SCATOLE**	Architecture	*arkeetet-**too**-ra* **ARCHITETTURA**
Bric a brac	*antee-**cal**-yay* **ANTICAGLIE**	Ceramics	*chair-**rar**-meekay* **CERAMICHE**
Bronzes	***bron**-zee* **BRONZI**	Drawings	*dee-**zay**-nee* **DISEGNI**
China	*porchel-**la**-nay* **PORCELLANE**	Etching	*akwa-**for**-tay* **ACQUAFORTE**
Coins	*mo-**net**-tay* **MONETE**	Frame	*cor-**nee**-chay* **CORNICE**
Dolls & toys	*bam-**bo**-lay ay jocka-**toh**-lee* **BAMBOLE E GIOCATTOLI**	Landscape	*pie-**sar**-jo* **PAESAGGIO**
Figures	*statoo-**wee**-nay* **STATUINE**	Minature	*meeneeya-**too**-ra* **MINIATURA**
Furniture	*mo-**beelee*** **MOBILI**	Oil painting	*pee-**too**-ra ah ol-yo* **PITTURA A OLIO**
Glass	***vay**-tro* **VETRO**	Portrait	*ree-**trar**-toh* **RITRATTO**
Militaria	*een-**sen**-yay meelee-**tar**-ree* **INSEGNE MILITARI**	Pottery	*tairray-**cot**-tay* **TERRECOTTE**
Musical instr	*stroo-**men**-tee moozee-**kar**-lee* **STRUMENTI MUSICALI**	Print	***stampa*** **STAMPA**
Scientific instruments	*stroo-**men**-tee shee-en-**tee**-feechee* **STRUMENTI SCIENTIFICI**	Sculpture	*scool-**too**-ra* **SCULTURA**
Silverware	*argentair-**ree**-ya* **ARGENTERIA**	Still life	*nar-**too**-ra **mor**-ta* **NATURA MORTA**
Veteran cars	*outoh an-**tee**-kay* **AUTO ANTICHE**	Textiles	***tess**-seelee* **TESSILI**
		Watercolour	*akwa-**rel**-lo* **ACQUARELLO**
broken	***rot**-toh* **ROTTO**		
cracked	*eencree-**nar**-toh* **INCRINATO**	(very) old	*(**mol**-toh) vec-keeyo* **(MOLTO) VECCHIO**
		classical	***clas**-seeko* **CLASSICO**
name	***no**-may* **NOME**	modern	*mo-**dair**-no* **MODERNO**
artist	*ar-**teess**-ta* **ARTISTA**	original	*oreejee-**nar**-lay* **ORIGINALE**
crate	***cass**-sa* **CASSA**	reproduction	*reeprodootsee-**yo**-nay* **RIPRODUZIONE**
insurance	*asseekoo-ratsee-**yo**-nay* **ASSICURAZIONE**	copy	***cop**-peeya* **COPIA**

clocks watches jewelry & minerals: 42B   **colours: 38A**

?

I	*ee-yo* **IO**	would like	*vor-ray-ee* **VORREI**
my	*eel mee-yo* **IL MIO**	want	*vwar-lay* **VUOLE**
you	*lay-ee* **LÈI**	have	*oh* **HO**
not	*non* **NON**	have	*ah* **HA**
no	*non* **NON**	do you have	*ah-vet-tay* **AVETE**
which	*kwar-lay* **QUALE**	is	*eh* **È**
when	*kwan-doh* **QUANDO**	are	*so-no* **SONO**
what	*koh-sa* **COSA**	is there	*chay* **C'È**

can I	*poss-o* **POSSO**		
can I have	*poss-o ah-vair-ray* **POSSO AVERE**		
can you	*pwoh* **PUÒ**		
Get	*pren-dair-ray* **PRENDERE**		
Repair	*reepar-rar-ray* **RIPARARE**		
will be Ready	*sar-rah pron-toh* **SARÀ PRONTO**		
See	*ved-dair-ray* **VEDERE**		
Send	*sped-dee-ray* **SPEDIRE**		
will Take	*pren-day* **PRENDE**		

how long	*kwan-toh tem-po* **QUANTO TEMPO**		
how many	*kwan-tee* **QUANTI**		

near	*vee-chee-no* **VICINO**	open	*a-pair-toh* **APERTO**	broken	*rot-toh* **ROTTO**
here	*kwee* **QUI**	closed	*kee-oo-zo* **CHIUSO**	small	*pee-ko-lo* **PICCOLO**
there	*lar* **LÀ**	deposit	*dep-poz-eeto* **DEPOSITO**	good	*bwoh-no* **BUONO**
this	*kwess-toh* **QUESTO**	receipt	*reechay-voo-ta* **RICEVUTA**	inexpensive	*eco-nom-meeco* **ECONOMICO**
these	*kwess-tee* **QUESTI**	name	*no-may* **NOME**	cheaper	*may-no car-ro* **MENO CARO**
		address	*eendee-reet-so* **INDIRIZZO**	better	*meel-yor-ray* **MIGLIORE**

THAT'S FINE	*va bay-nay* **VA BENE**
HOW MUCH IS (THAT)?	*kwan-toh coss-ta* **QUANTO COSTA?**

bigger	*pee-yoo gran-day* **PIÙ GRANDE**
smaller	*pee-yoo pee-ko-lo* **PIÙ PICCOLO**
alternative	*altairna-tee-va* **ALTERNATIVA**
simpler	*pee-yoo sem-plee-chay* **PIÙ SEMPLICE**
similar	*see-meelay* **SIMILE**

at	by	for	in	of	to
al	*dee*	*pair*	*dee*	*dee*	*ah*
al	**di**	**per**	**di**	**di**	**a**

money: 50A   time: 60

WATCH	*orro-**lod**-jo* **OROLOGIO**		MATERIAL	*matairree-**yar**-lay* **MATERIALE**
Alarm clock	*svel-ya* **SVEGLIA**		Amber	*am-bra* **AMBRA**
Battery	*pee-la* **PILA**		Ceramic	*chair-**rar**-meeka* **CERAMICA**
Clock	*orro-**lod**-jo* **OROLOGIO**		Chromium	*kro-mo* **CROMO**
Glass	*vay-tro* **VETRO**		Copper	*rar-may* **RAME**
Strap	*cheentoo-**ree**-no* **CINTURINO**		Crystal	*crees-**tar**-lo* **CRISTALLO**
Winder	*keeya-**vet**-ta* **CHIAVETTA**		Diamond	*deeya-**man**-tay* **DIAMANTE**
			Ebony	*ebb-arno* **EBANO**
JEWELRY	*joy-**yel**-lee* **GIOIELLI**		Emerald	*smair-**ral**-doh* **SMERALDO**
Bracelet	*bratcha-**let**-toh* **BRACCIALETTO**		Enamel	*smal-toh* **SMALTO**
Brooch	*spee-la* **SPILLA**		(cut) Glass	*vay-tro (eetal-**yar**-toh)* **VETRO (INTAGLIATO)**
Cameo	*cam-**may**-yo* **CAMMEO**		Gold (plate)	*(plac-**car**-toh d') or-ro* **(PLACCATO D') ORO**
Chain	*catten-**nee**-na* **CATENINA**		Ivory	*av-**vor**-reeyo* **AVORIO**
Clip	*fair-**marl**-yo* **FERMAGLIO**		Jade	*jar-da* **GIADA**
Earrings	*oray-**kee**-nee* **ORECCHINI**		Onyx	*on-eechay* **ONICE**
Necklace	*col-**lar**-na* **COLLANA**		Pearl	*pair-la* **PERLA**
Pendant	*pen-**den**-tay* **PENDENTE**		Pewter	*pel-tro* **PELTRO**
Ring	*an-**nel**-lo* **ANELLO**		Platinium	*plat-teeno* **PLATINO**
			Ruby	*roo-**bee**-no* **RUBINO**
souvenir	*ree-**cor**-doh* **RICORDO**		Sapphire	*tsa-**fee**-ro* **ZAFFIRO**
present	*reh-**gar**-lo* **REGALO**		Silver (plate)	*(plac-**car**-toh d') ar-**jen**-toh* **(PLACCATO D') ARGENTO**
real	*vair-ro* **VERO**		Stainless steel	*at-**chee**-yo eenosee-**dar**-beelay* **ACCIAIO INOSSIDABILE**
carats	*ka-**rat**-tee* **CARATI**		Turquoise	*toor-**kay**-zay* **TURCHESE**

colours: 38A

?

I *ee-yo* **IO**

my *eel mee-yo* **IL MIO**

you *lay-ee* **LEI**

not *non* **NON**

no *non* **NON**

which *kwar-lay* **QUALE**

when *kwan-doh* **QUANDO**

what *koh-sa* **COSA**

what time *kay or-ra* **CHE ORA**

would like *vor-ray-ee* **VORREI**	can I *poss-o* **POSSO**
want *vwar-lay* **VUOLE**	can I have *poss-o ah-vair-ray* **POSSO AVERE**
have *oh* **HO**	can you *pwoh* **PUÒ**
have *ah* **HA**	Get *pren-dair-ray* **PRENDERE**
do you have *ah-vet-tay* **AVETE**	Process *sveeloo-par-ray* **SVILUPPARE**
is *eh* **È**	(and) Print *(ay) stam-par-ray* **(E) STAMPARE**
are *so-no* **SONO**	will be Ready *sar-rah pron-toh* **SARÀ PRONTO**
is there *chay* **C'È**	Repair *reepar-rar-ray* **RIPARARE**
	Show me *mee moss-tree* **MI MOSTRI**
	will Take *pren-day* **PRENDE**

how long *kwan-toh tem-po* **QUANTO TEMPO**

how many *kwan-tee* **QUANTI**

near *vee-chee-no* **VICINO**

here *kwee* **QUI**

this *kwess-toh* **QUESTO**

these *kwess-tee* **QUESTI**

nearest *pee-yoo vee-chee-no* **PIÙ VICINO**

open *a-pair-toh* **APERTO**

closed *kee-oo-zo* **CHIUSO**

receipt *reechay-voo-ta* **RICEVUTA**

name *no-may* **NOME**

address *eendee-reet-so* **INDIRIZZO**

good *bwoh-no* **BUONO**

inexpensive *econ-nom-eeco* **ECONOMICO**

alternative *altairna-tee-va* **ALTERNATIVA**

too *trop-po* **TROPPO**

more *pee-yoo* **PIÙ**

light *kee-yar-ro* **CHIARO**

dark *scoo-ro* **SCURO**

THAT'S FINE *va bay-nay* **VA BENE**

HOW MUCH IS (THAT)? *kwan-toh coss-ta* **QUANTO COSTA?**

broken *rot-toh* **ROTTO**

jammed *bloc-kar-toh* **BLOCCATO**

working *foontsee-yo-na* **FUNZIONA**

at	by	for	from	of	to
al	*een*	*pair*	*dah*	*dee*	*ah*
AL	**IN**	**PER**	**DA**	**DI**	**A**

money: 50A   time: 60

FILM	*pel-lee-cola* **PELLICOLA**		EQUIPMENT	*ekweeparja-men-toh* **EQUIPAGGIAMENTO**
110 cartridge	*chentoh dee-yay-chee ro-toh-lo* **110 ROTOLO**		Battery	*pee-la* **PILA**
120	*chentoh-ven-tee* **120**		Cable release	*fee-lo dee scar-toh* **FILO DI SCATTO**
127	*chentoh-ven-tee set-tay* **127**		Camera	*mak-keena foto-gra-feeka* **MACCHINA FOTOGRAFICA**
35mm	*trenta-cheen-kway mee-lee-metree* **35mm**		Filter	*feel-tro* **FILTRO**
620	*saychento-ven-tee* **620**		Flash bulb	*lampa-dee-na pair eel flash* **LAMPADINA PER IL FLASH**
8mm	*ot-toh mee-lee-metree* **8mm**		Flash cube	*koo-bo flash* **CUBO FLASH**
super 8	*soo-pair ot-toh* **SUPER 8**		Focus	*foo-woh-ko* **FUOCO**
16mm	*sed-eechee mee-lee-metree* **16mm**		Lens	*obbeeyet-tee-vo* **OBIETTIVO**
polaroid film	*pel-lee-cola polaroid* **PELLICOLA POLAROID**		Lightmeter	*espo-zee-metro* **ESPOSIMETRO**
video cassette	*vee-dayo cass-set-ta* **VIDEO CASSETTA**		Movie camera	*cheenay-pray-za* **CINEPRESA**
	12 20 24 36		Rewind mechanism	*meckan-neez-mo dee reeya-voljee-men-toh* **MECCANISMO DI RIAVVOLGIMENTO**
exposures	*poz* **POSES**		Shutter	*ottoo-rat-tor-ray* **OTTURATORE**
ASA/DIN	*ar-sah/deen* **ASA/DIN**		Tripod	*trep-pyay-dee* **TREPPIEDI**
fast	*rar-peedo* **RAPIDO**		Viewfinder	*mee-ree-no* **MIRINO**
fine grain	*grar-na fee-nay* **GRANA FINE**			
for indoors	*pair een-tair-no* **PER INTERNO**		PRINTS	*cop-peeyay* **COPIE**
for outdoor	*pair ess-tair-no* **PER ESTERNO**		negative	*negga-tee-va* **NEGATIVA**
			gloss finish	*car-ta loo-cheeda* **CARTA LUCIDA**
black & white	*bee-yang-co ay nair-ro* **BIANCO E NERO**		matt finish	*car-ta op-par-ka* **CARTA OPACA**
colour prints	*cop-peeyay collor-rar-tay* **COPIE COLORATE**		enlargement	*eengrandee-men-toh* **INGRANDIMENTO**
colour slides	*deeyapozee-tee-vay collor-rar-tay* **DIAPOSITIVE COLORATE**		size	*mee-zoo-ra* **MISURA**

colours: 38A

?		
I	*ee-yo*	**IO**
my	*eel mee-yo*	**IL MIO**
you	*lay-ee*	**LEI**
not	*non*	**NON**
no	*non*	**NON**
which	*kwar-lay*	**QUALE**
where	*doh-vay*	**DOVE**
when	*kwan-doh*	**QUANDO**
what	*koh-sa*	**COSA**

would like	*vor-ray-ee*	**VORREI**	can I	*poss-o*	**POSSO**
want	*vwar-lay*	**VUOLE**	can I have	*poss-o ah-vair-ray*	**POSSO AVERE**
have	*oh*	**HO**	can you	*pwoh*	**PUÒ**
have	*ha*	**AH**	Get	*pren-dair-ray*	**PRENDERE**
do you have	*ah-vet-tay*	**AVETE**	Listen to	*ascol-tar-ray ah*	**ASCOLTARE A**
is	*eh*	**È**	will be Ready	*sar-rah pron-toh*	**SARÀ PRONTO**
are	*so-no*	**SONO**	Recommend	*raccoman-dar-ray*	**RACCOMANDARE**
is there	*chay*	**C'È**	Repair	*reepar-rar-ray*	**RIPARARE**
			See	*ved-dair-ray*	**VEDERE**

how many	*kwan-tee*	**QUANTI**	nearest	*pee-yoo vee-chee-no*	**PIÙ VICINO**	good	*bwoh-no*	**BUONO**
how works	*ko-may foontsee-yo-na*	**COME FUNZIONA**	open	*a-pair-toh*	**APERTO**	small	*pee-ko-lo*	**PICCOLO**
near	*vee-chee-no*	**VICINO**	closed	*kee-oo-zo*	**CHIUSO**	inexpensive	*econ-nom-eeco*	**ECONOMICO**
here	*kwee*	**QUI**	broken	*rot-toh*	**ROTTO**	alternative	*altairna-tee-va*	**ALTERNATIVA**
this	*kwess-toh*	**QUESTO**	receipt	*reechay-voo-ta*	**RICEVUTA**	similar	*see-meelay*	**SIMILE**
these	*kwess-tee*	**QUESTI**	name	*no-may*	**NOME**	too	*mol-toh*	**MOLTO**
						more	*pee-yoo*	**PIÙ**

THAT'S FINE	*va bay-nay*	**VA BENE**
HOW MUCH IS (THAT)?	*kwan-toh coss-ta*	**QUANTO COSTA?**

local	*lo-car-lay*	**LOCALE**
regional	*rejeeyo-nar-lay*	**REGIONALE**
national	*natseeyo-nar-lay*	**NAZIONALE**

at	by	for	from	of	to
al	*dee*	*pair*	*dah*	*dee*	*ah*
AL	**DI**	**PER**	**DA**	**DI**	**A**

ELECTRICAL	*el-let-reeco*	RECORDS & TAPES	*dees-kee ay cas-set-tay*
	ELETTRICO		**DISCHI E CASSETTE**
Adaptor	*pet-so dee ra-kor-doh*	(blank) Cassette	*cas-set-tay (vwoh-tay)*
	PEZZO DI RACCORDO		**CASSETTE (VUOTE)**
Amplifier	*ampleefeecat-tor-ray*	Record	*dees-ko*
	AMPLIFICATORE		**DISCO**
Battery	*pee-la*	Single	*kwarranta-cheen-kway*
	PILA		*jee-ree*
Cas'tte recorder	*redjeestra-tor-ray*		**45 GIRI**
	REGISTRATORE	LP	*traynta-tray jee-ree*
Alarm clock	*svel-ya*		**33 GIRI**
	SVEGLIA	Stylus	*stee-lo*
Hair drier	*fon*		**STILO**
	FON	Stereo	*stairrayo-fon-eeko*
Iron	*fair-ro dah stee-ro*		**STEREOFONICO**
	FERRO DA STIRO		
Kettle	*bollee-tor-ray*		
	BOLLITORE		
Light bulb/globe	*lampa-dee-na*	Classical music	*moo-zeeka class-eeka*
	LAMPADINA		**MUSICA CLASSICA**
Percolator	*mak-keena dah caf-fay*	Jazz	*jazz*
	MACCHINA DA CAFFÈ		**JAZZ**
Plug	*spee-na*	Folk music	*moo-zeeka folk*
	SPINA		**MUSICA FOLK**
Radio	*rar-deeyo*	Light music	*moo-zeeka lay-jair-ra*
	RADIO		**MUSICA LEGGERA**
Record player	*jee-ra-deess-kee*	Pop music	*moo-zeeka pop*
	GIRADISCHI		**MUSICA POP**
Shaver	*ra-zo-eeyo*	Opera	*op-pair-ra*
	RASOIO		**OPERA**
Television	*televee-zor-ray*		
	TELEVISORE		
Transformer	*trazforma-tor-ray*		
	TRASFORMATORE	choral	*cor-rar-lee*
			CORALI
		group	*groo-po*
			GRUPPO
for camping	*pair cam-ped-jo*	instrumental	*stroomen-tar-lay*
	PER CAMPEGGIO		**STRUMENTALE**
for car	*pair mak-keena*	male	*mas-kee-lay*
	PER MACCHINA		**MASCHILE**
for travelling	*dah vee-yar-jo*	female	*femmee-nee-lay*
	DA VIAGGIO		**FEMMINILE**
portable	*por-tar-teelay*	orchestral	*seen-fon-neeka*
	PORTATILE		**SINFONICA**
voltage	*vol-tar-jo*	singer	*can-tan-tay*
	VOLTAGGIO		**CANTANTE**

?

I	*ee-yo* **IO**	want	*vol-yo* **VOGLIO**
my	*eel mee-yo* **IL MIO**	want	*vwar-lay* **VUOLE**
me	*may* **ME**	have	*oh* **HO**
you	*lay-ee* **LEI**	have	*ah* **HA**
your	*eel soo-oh* **IL SUO**	do you have	*ah-vet-tay* **AVETE**
he	*lwee* **LUI**	am	*so-no* **SONO**
she	*lay-ee* **LEI**	is	*eh* **È**
his	*eel soo-oh* **IL SUO**	are	*so-no* **SONO**
her	*la soo-ah* **LA SUA**	is there	*chay* **C'È**
not	*non* **NON**		
no	*non* **NON**		

can I	*poss-o* **POSSO**
can I have	*poss-o ah-vair-ray* **POSSO AVERE**
can you	*pwoh* **PUÒ**
Come back	*reetor-nar-ray* **RITORNARE**
Make	*prepar-rar-ray* **PREPARARE**
will be Ready	*sar-rah pron-toh* **SARÀ PRONTO**
Recommend	*racoman-dar-ray* **RACCOMANDARE**
Take	*pren-dair-ray* **PRENDERE**
Tell me	*mee dee-ka* **MI DICA**
Wait	*aspet-tar-ray* **ASPETTARE**

which	*kwar-lay* **QUALE**	nearest	*pee-yoo vee-chee-no* **PIÙ VICINO**	wife	*mol-yay* **MOGLIE**
when	*kwan-doh* **QUANDO**	all-night	*dee toor-no* **DI TURNO**	husband	*ma-ree-toh* **MARITO**
what	*koh-sa* **COSA**	open	*a-pair-toh* **APERTO**	friend	*a-mee-co* **AMICO**
what time	*kay or-ra* **CHE ORA**	closed	*kee-oo-zo* **CHIUSO**	child	*bam-bee-no* **BAMBINO**
how many	*kwan-tee* **QUANTI**	prescription	*ree-chet-ta* **RICETTA**	dentist	*den-tees-ta* **DENTISTA**
how often	*kwan-tay vol-tay* **QUANTE VOLTE**	name	*no-may* **NOME**	doctor	*med-eeco* **MEDICO**

near	*vee-chee-no* **VICINO**
here	*kwee* **QUI**
this	*kwess-toh* **QUESTO**

HOW MUCH IS (THAT)? *kwan-toh coss-ta* **QUANTO COSTA?**

at	by	for	from	in	on	to
al **AL**	*ah* **A**	*pair* **PER**	*dah* **DA**	*een* **IN**	*soo* **SU**	*ah* **A**

pharmaceuticals: 46A   toiletries: 46B   money: 50A   time: 60

some	*kwal*-kay **QUALCHE**
something	*kwal*-co-sa **QUALCOSA**
safe	see-**koo**-ro **SICURO**
much	*mol*-toh **MOLTO**
high	*al*-toh **ALTO**
low	*bass*-so **BASSO**
more	pee-**yoo** **PIÙ**
less	*may*-no **MENO**
hot	*cal*-doh **CALDO**
cold	*fray*-doh **FREDDO**

INSTRUCTIONS — eestrootsee-yo-nee **ISTRUZIONI**

dosage	*doss*-say **DOSE**
teaspoonfulls	kookeeya-**ee**-no dah tay pee-**yay**-no **CUCCHIAINO DA TÈ PIENO**
times daily	*vol*-ta al *jor*-no **VOLTE AL GIORNO**
swallow whole	een-gheeyo-**tee**-ray een-**tair**-ray **INGHIOTTIRE INTERE**
every . . . hours	*on*-yee . . . *or*-ray **OGNI . . . . ORE**
before	*pree*-ma **PRIMA**
after	*dor*-po **DOPO**
between	frah **FRA**
with	con **CON**
meals	*pas*-tee **PASTI**
water	*ak*-wa **ACQUA**
in morning	al mat-**tee**-no **AL MATTINO**
at night	dee *not*-tay **DI NOTTE**
using toilet	an-**dar**-ray alla toy-**let**-tay **ANDARE ALLA TOILETTE**

SYMPTOMS — seen-**toh**-mee **SINTOMI**

Asthma	*az*-ma **ASMA**
Chapped skin	*pel*-lay screpol-**lar**-ta **PELLE SCREPOLATA**
(a) Cold	raffred-**dor**-ray **RAFFREDDORE**
Constipation	costeepatsee-yo-nay **COSTIPAZIONE**
Cough	*toss*-say **TOSSE**
Diarrhea	deeyar-**ray**-ya **DIARREA**
Hay fever	*feb*-bray dah fee-**yay**-no **FEBBRE DA FIENO**
Headache	mal dee *tess*-ta **MAL DI TESTA**
Indigestion	eendeejestee-yo-nay **INDIGESTIONE**
Infection	eenfetsee-yo-nay **INFEZIONE**
Inflammation	eenfeeyamatsee-yo-nay **INFIAMMAZIONE**
Insect bite	poon-**too**-ra deen-**set**-toh **PUNTURA D'INSETTO**
Itch	proo-**ree**-toh **PRURITO**
Nausea	*now*-saya **NAUSEA**
Pain	dol-**lor**-ray **DOLORE**
Rash	*sfo*-go **SFOGO**
Sore throat	mal dee *go*-la **MAL DI GOLA**
Stomach ache	mal dee *stom*-marco **MAL DI STOMACO**
Sunburn	scotta-**too**-ra sol-**lar**-ray **SCOTTATURA SOLARE**
(a) Temperature	la *feb*-bray **LA FEBBRE**
Toothache	mal dee *den*-tee **MAL DI DENTI**
Travel sickness	mal dee vee-**yar**-jo **MAL DI VIAGGIO**

| dentist: 52 | doctor: 53 | wounds & damage: 54B | body parts: 55 |

PHARMACEUTICALS	*farmar-chay-ooteechee* **FARMACEUTICI**		Insulin	*eensoo-lee-na* **INSULINA**
Analgesic	*annal-jez-eeko* **ANALGESICO**		Iodine	*teen-too-ra dee ee-yo-deeyo* **TINTURA DI IODIO**
Anti-histamine	*anti-eesta-mee-neeco* **ANTI-ISTAMINICO**		Laxative	*lassa-tee-vo* **LASSATIVO**
Antiseptic	*antee-set-teeco* **ANTISETTICO**		Medicine	*medee-chee-na* **MEDICINA**
Aspirins	*aspee-ree-nay* **ASPIRINE**		Mouthwash	*deeseenfet-tan-tay pair la bok-ka* **DISINFETTANTE PER LA BOCCA**
Bandages	*ben-day* **BENDE**		Sedative	*sedat-tee-vo* **SEDATIVO**
(crepe/gauze)	*(cres-par-tay/gart-sa)* **(CRESPATE GARZA)**		Sleeping pills	*son-nee-fairee* **SONNIFERI**
Bands-Aids	*chair-rot-toh* **CEROTTO**		Stomach pills	*pee-lo-lay pair lo stom-maco* **PILLOLE PER LO STOMACO**
Calamine	*cala-mee-na* **CALAMINA**		Throat lozenges	*pas-tee-kay pair la go-la* **PASTICCHE PER LA GOLA**
Contraceptives	*contrachet-tee-vo* **CONTRACCETTIVO**		Vitamins	*veeta-mee-nay* **VITAMINE**
(pill/sheaths)	*(pee-lo-la /prezairva-tee-vee)* **(PILLOLA PRESERVATIVI)**			
Corn plasters	*ca-lee-foogo* **CALLIFUGO**		Capsules	*com-press-say* **COMPRESSE**
Cotton wool	*cot-toh-nay ee-dro-feelo* **COTONE IDROFILO**		Cream	*cray-ma* **CREMA**
Cough drops	*got-chay pair la toss-say* **GOCCE PER LA TOSSE**		Drops	*got-chay* **GOCCE**
Decongestant	*deckon-jesteeyo-nan-tay* **DECONGESTIONANTE**		Lozenges	*pas-tee-kay* **PASTICCHE**
Diabetic loz'gs	*lot-san-gay pair deeya-bet-eechee* **LOZANGHE PER DIABETICI**		Lotion	*low-tsee-yo-nay* **LOZIONE**
Disinfectant	*deeseenfet-tan-tay* **DISINFETTANTE**		Ointment	*oong-gwen-toh* **UNGUENTO**
Ear drops	*got-chay pair ley or-ray-keeyay* **GOCCE PER LE ORECCHIE**		Powder	*pol-vair-ray* **POLVERE**
Elastoplast	*chair-rot-toh* **CEROTTO**		Suppositories	*soo-poss-tay* **SUPPOSTE**
Eye drops	*collee-ree-yo* **COLLIRIO**		Tablets	*pas-teel-yay* **PASTIGLIE**
Gargle	*lee-kweedo pair gargar-rees-mee* **LIQUIDO PER GARGARISMI**		Tonic	*ton-neeko* **TONICO**
Gauze	*gart-sa* **GARZA**			
Insect repel'nt	*eensettee-foo-go* **INSETTIFUGO**		Thermometer	*tair-mom-aytro* **TERMOMETRO**

	TOILETRIES	*cos-met-eechee* **COSMETICI**	
Aftershave	*dorpo-bar-bar* **DOPOBARBA**	Nail scissors	*forbee-chee-nay pair lay oong-gheeyay* **FORBICINE PER LE UNGHIE**
Bath salts	*sar-lee dah ban-yo* **SALI DA BAGNO**	Nail varnish	*smal-toh (pair oong-gheeyay)* **SMALTO (PER UNGHIE)**
Brush	*spat-sola pair ka-pel-lee* **SPAZZOLA PER CAPELLI**	Nail varnish remover	*achay-toh-nay* **ACETONE**
Cleansing cream	*cray-ma dettair-jen-tay* **CREMA DETERGENTE**	Nappies	*panno-lee-nee* **PANNOLINI**
Comb	*pet-teenay* **PETTINE**	Perfume	*prof-foo-mo* **PROFUMO**
Cologne	*ak-wa dee col-lon-eeya* **ACQUA DI COLONIA**	Powder	*chee-preeya* **CIPRIA**
Curlers	*beego-dee-nee* **BIGODINI**	Razor	*ra-zo-eeyo* **RASOIO**
Deodorant	*dayo-dor-ran-tay* **DEODORANTE**	Razor blades	*lam-met-tay dah bar-ba* **LAMETTE DA BARBA**
Diapers	*panno-lee-nee* **PANNOLINI**	Rouge	*bel-let-toh* **BELLETTO**
Eye pencil	*ma-tee-ta pair ock-kee* **MATITA PER OCCHI**	Safety pins	*spee-lay dee seekoo-ret-sa* **SPILLE DI SICUREZZA**
Eye shadow	*ree-mel* **RIMMEL**	Sanitary towels/napkins	*assor-ben-tee* **ASSORBENTI**
Foot powder	*pol-vair-ray pair pee-yay-dee* **POLVERE PER PIEDI**	Setting lotion	*low-tsee-yo-nay feessa-tee-va* **LOZIONE FISSATIVA**
Foundation cream	*fon-doh teen-ta* **FONDO TINTA**	Shampoo	*sham-poh* **SHAMPO**
Hair grips	*for-chair-lay* **FORCELLE**	Shaving cream	*cray-ma dah bar-ba* **CREMA DA BARBA**
hair lacquer	*lac-ka* **LACCA**	Soap	*sap-poh-nay* **SAPONE**
Hair tinting	*sfooma-too-ra* **SFUMATURA**	Suntan-cream/oil	*cray-ma/ol-yo -sol-lar-ray* **CREMA OLIO -SOLARE**
Hand cream	*cray-ma pair lay mar-nee* **CREMA PER LE MANI**	Talc	*tal-co* **TALCO**
Lipstick	*ross-set-toh* **ROSSETTO**	Tissues	*fatso-let-tee-nee dee car-ta* **FAZZOLETTINI DI CARTA**
Mascara	*mass-car-ra* **MASCARA**	Toilet paper	*car-ta ee-jen-eeka* **CARTA IGIENICA**
Mirror	*speck-yo* **SPECCHIO**	Toothbrush	*spatso-lee-no dah den-tee* **SPAZZOLINO DA DENTI**
Moisturiser cream	*cray-ma eedra-tan-tay* **CREMA IDRATANTE**	Toothpaste	*dentee-free-cho* **DENTIFRICIO**
Nail file	*lee-ma dah oong-gheeyay* **LIMA DA UNGHIE**	Tweezers	*peent-set-tay* **PINZETTE**

?	I	*ee-yo* **IO**
my	*eel mee-yo* **IL MIO**
you	*lay-ee* **LEI**
your	*eel soo-oh* **IL SUO**
not	*non* **NON**
no	*non* **NON**
which	*kwar-lay* **QUALE**
where	*doh-vay* **DOVE**
when	*kwan-doh* **QUANDO**
what	*koh-sa* **COSA**
what time	*kay or-ra* **CHE ORA**
how long	*kwan-toh tem-po* **QUANTO TEMPO**
how many	*kwan-tee* **QUANTI**
near	*vee-chee-no* **VICINO**
here	*kwee* **QUI**
there	*lar* **LÀ**
this	*kwess-toh* **QUESTO**
these	*kwess-tee* **QUESTI**

would like	*vor-ray-ee* **VORREI**		can I	*poss-o* **POSSO**
want	*vwar-lay* **VUOLE**		can I have	*poss-o ah-vair-ray* **POSSO AVERE**
have	*oh* **HO**		can you	*pwoh* **PUÒ**
have	*ah* **HA**		will Arrive	*arreevair-ra* **ARRIVERÀ**
do you have	*ah-vet-tay* **AVETE**		Go	*an-dar-ray* **ANDARE**
			Post	*eemboo-car-ray* **IMBUCARE**
is	*eh* **È**		Send	*man-dar-ray* **MANDARE**
are	*so-no* **SONO**		Sign	*fer-mar-ray* **FIRMARE**
is there	*chay* **C'È**		will Take	*pren-day* **PRENDE**

nearest	*pee-yoo vee-chee-no* **PIÙ VICINO**		each	*loo-no* **L'UNO**
post box	*cas-set-ta del-lay let-tairra* **CASSETTA DELLE LETTERE**		per word	*on-yee par-ro-la* **OGNI PAROLA**
open	*a-pair-toh* **APERTO**		total	*toh-tar-lay* **TOTALE**
closed	*kee-oo-zo* **CHIUSO**		in Italian	*een eetal-yar-no* **IN ITALIANO**

HOW MUCH IS (THAT)? *kwan-toh coss-ta* **QUANTO COSTA?**

FERMO POSTA = POST RESTANTE/GENERAL DELIVERY
FRANCOBOLLI = STAMPS
PACCHI = PARCELS
VAGLIA POSTALE = MONEY ORDERS

	and	any	at	by	for	from	to
	ay **E**	*day* **DEI**	*al* **AL**	*pair* **PER**	*pair* **PER**	*dah* **DA**	*ah* **A**

bank: 49　　**money: 50A**

first	*pree-mo* **PRIMO**		Air mail	*vee-ya ah-ee-raya* **VIA AEREA**
last	*ool-teemo* **ULTIMO**		Express	*ess-press-so* **ESPRESSO**
next	*pross-eemo* **PROSSIMO**		parcel post	*pac-kee* **PACCHI**
			Registered	*asseekoo-rar-ta* **ASSICURATA**
days	*jor-nee* **GIORNI**		Recorded delivery	*raccoman-dar-ta* **RACCOMANDATA**
weeks	*settee-mar-nay* **SETTIMANE**		Surface mail	*poss-ta nor-mar-lay* **POSTA NORMALE**
today	*od-jee* **OGGI**			
tomorrow	*dom-mar-nee* **DOMANI**			
morning	*mat-tee-no* **MATTINO**		Customs	*doh-gar-na* **DOGANA**
afternoon	*pomair-reed-jo* **POMERIGGIO**		Delivery	*con-sairn-ya* **CONSEGNA**
			General delivery	*fair-mo poss-ta* **FERMO POSTA**
Letter	*let-taira* **LETTERA**		Intn'l money order	*val-ya eentair-natseeyo-nar-nay* **VAGLIA INTERNAZIONALE**
Form	*mod-doolo* **MODULO**		Philatelic bureau	*spor-tell-lo feela-tay-leeko* **SPORTELLO FILATELICO**
Mail	*poss-ta* **POSTA**		Poste restante	*fair-mo poss-ta* **FERMO POSTA**
Parcel	*pac-ko* **PACCO**			
Post card	*carto-lee-na* **CARTOLINA**			
Protective envelope	*boo-sta eembot-tee-ta* **BUSTA IMBOTTITA**		country	*par-ay-zay* **PAESE**
Stamps	*franco-bol-lee* **FRANCOBOLLI**		Australia	*ows-trar-leeya* **AUSTRALIA**
Tele-facsimile	*tellay fac-see-meelay* **TELEFACSIMILE**		Britain	*bret-tar-nya* **BRETAGNA**
Telegram	*telay-grar-ma* **TELEGRAMMA**		Canada	*canna-dah* **CANADÀ**
Telex	*tel-lex* **TELEX**		Ireland	*ear-lan-da* **IRLANDA**
			New Zealand	*nwor-va tsay-lan-da* **NUOVA ZELANDA**
name	*no-may* **NOME**		Sth Africa	*sood ar-freeka* **SUD AFRICA**
address	*eendee-reet-so* **INDIRIZZO**		USA	*star-tee oo-nee-tee* **STATI UNITI**

To avoid coin-feeding, long distance calls are best made from Local Telephone Centres. Public phones are operated by either coins or telephone tokens inserted before dialling. Tokens can be purchased from cashiers in bars or restaurants etc., or from change machines. In Italian, phone numbers are stated in pairs, eg. 2386 would be *twenty-three, eighty-six*, however single numbers will probably be understood.

?

I	*ee-yo* **IO**	want	*vol-yo* **VOGLIO**	can I	*poss-o* **POSSO**
my	*eel mee-yo* **IL MIO**	want	*vwar-lay* **VUOLE**	can I have	*poss-o ah-vair-ray* **POSSO AVERE**
you	*lay-ee* **LEI**	have	*oh* **HO**	Call again	*kee-yar-mee an-cor-ra* **CHIAMI ANCORA**
who	*kee* **CHI**	have	*ah* **HA**	Dial	*keeya-mar-ray* **CHIAMARE**
		is	*eh* **È**	(direct)	*(dee-reta-men-tay)* **(DIRETTAMENTE)**
not	*non* **NON**	are	*so-no* **SONO**	Make	*far-ray* **FARE**
no	*non* **NON**	is there	*chay* **C'È**	Speak	*par-lar-ray* **PARLARE**
				Tell me	*mee dee-ka* **MI DICA**
where	*doh-vay* **DOVE**	can you	*pwoh* **PUÒ**	Use	*oo-zar-ray* **USARE**
when	*kwan-doh* **QUANDO**				
what	*koh-sa* **COSA**				

DO YOU SPEAK ENGLISH?   *par-la eeng-glay-zee?* **PARLA INGLESE?**

DOES ANYONE THERE SPEAK ENGLISH?	*chay kwal-koo-no kay par-la eeng-glay-zay?* **C'E QUALCUNO CHI PARLA INGLESE?**

how long	*kwan-toh tem-po* **QUANTO TEMPO**
how many	*kwan-tee* **QUANTI**

SPEAK VERY SLOWLY   *par-lee lenta-men-tay* **PARLI LENTAMENTE**

I DON'T UNDERSTAND   *non ka-peess-co* **NON CAPISCO**

near	*vee-chee-no* **VICINO**
here	*kwee* **QUI**
there	*lar* **LÀ**
this	*kwess-toh* **QUESTO**
that	*kwel-lo* **QUELLO**

SAY AGAIN VERY SLOWLY   *lo ree-pet-ta lenta-men-tay* **LO RIPETA LENTAMENTE**

HOW MUCH IS THAT/IT?   *kwan-toh coss-ta?* **KWANTO COSTA?**

and	at	for	from	in	to
ay	*al*	*pair*	*dah*	*een*	*ah*
E	**AL**	**PER**	**DA**	**IN**	**A**

the code	eel pref-**ee**-so	IL PREFISSO
the name	eel no-may	IL NOME
the number	eel noo-mairro	IL NUMERO
later	pee-yoo tar-dee	PIÙ TARDI
afterwards	dor-po	DOPO
per	al	AL
minute	mee-noo-toh	MINUTO
International call	telefon-nar-ta eentair-natseeyo-nar-lay	TELEFONATA INTERNAZIONALE
Telephone call	telefon-nar-ta	TELEFONATA
Person to person call	telefon-nar-ta pairson-nar-lay	TELEFONATA PERSONALE
Reverse charge/ Collect call	spay-za al reechay-ven-tay	SPESA AL RICEVENTE
the Extension	lah lee-naya een-tair-na	LA LINEA INTERNA
the Operator	eel sentra-lee-no	IL CENTRALINO
the Telephone	eel tel-lef-onno	IL TELEFONO
Telephone Box	ca-bee-na tele-fon-eeka	CABINA TELEFONICA
Telephone Directory	el-len-co tele-fon-eeco	ELENCO TELEFONICO
Telephone Tokens	jet-toh-nay tele-fon-eeco	GETTONE TELEFONICO
Australia	ow-stra-leeya	AUSTRALIA
Britain	bret-tar-nya	BRETAGNA
Canada	canna-dah	CANADÀ
Ireland	ear-lan-da	IRLANDA
New Zealand	nwor-va tsay-lan-da	NUOVA ZELANDA
Sth Africa	sood ar-freeka	SUD AFRICA
USA	star-tee oo-neetee	STATI UNITI

THE OPERATOR OR PERSON AT
THE OTHER END MIGHT SAY:

0	tsair-ro	
1	oo-no	
2	doo-way	
3	tray	
4	kway-tro	
5	cheen-kway	
6	say-ee	
7	set-tay	
8	ot-toh	
9	no-vay	

Pronunciation	English
pron-toh	Hello
telefon-nar-ta pair lay-ee	Telephone call for you
kay noo-mairro kee-yar-ma?	What number do you want?
eel soo-oh no-may?	What's your name?
eel soo-oh noo-mairro?	What's your number
ress-tee een lee-naya	Hold the line
po-tay-tay par-lar-lay	Go ahead please
la lee-naya ay ockoo-par-ta	The line's engaged/busy
non rees-pon-day	There's no reply
noo-mairro sbal-yar-toh	Wrong number

emergency phone numbers vary from place to place

? I *ee-yo*
IO

would like	*vor-ray-ee* **VORREI**		is there	*chay* **C'È**

my *eel mee-yo*
IL MIO

you *lay-ee*
LEI

| | want | *vwar-lay* **VUOLE** | | Arrange | *organeet-sar-ray* **ORGANIZZARE** |

your *eel soo-oh*
IL SUO

have *oh*
HO

Cash *eencass-sar-ray*
INCASSARE

have *ah*
HA

Change *cambee-yar-ray*
CAMBIARE

Charge *coss-tar-ray*
COSTARE

not *non*
NON

do you have *ah-vet-tay*
AVETE

Come back *reetor-nar-ray*
RITORNARE

no *non*
NON

Expect *aspet-tar-ray*
ASPETTARE

is *eh*
È

which *kwar-lay*
QUALE

are *so-no*
SONO

Pay *pa-gar-ray*
PAGARE

where *doh-vay*
DOVE

Receive *reechay-vair-ray*
RICEVERE

when *kwan-doh*
QUANDO

can I *poss-o*
POSSO

will be Ready *sar-rah pron-toh*
SARÀ PRONTO

what *koh-sa*
COSA

can I have *poss-o ah-vair-ray*
POSSO AVERE

Sign *feer-mar-ray*
FIRMARE

can you *pwoh*
PUÒ

Wait *aspet-tar-ray*
ASPETTARE

what time *kay or-ra*
CHE ORA

	nearest	*pee-yoo vee-chee-no* **PIÙ VICINO**	each	*loo-no* **L'UNO**

how *koh-may*
COME

bank *ban-ca*
BANCA

receipt *reechay-voo-ta*
RICEVUTA

how much *kwan-toh*
QUANTO

change bureau *cam-beeyo*
CAMBIO

money *den-nar-ro*
DENARO

open *a-pair-toh*
APERTO

name *no-may*
NOME

near *vee-chee-no*
VICINO

closed *kee-oo-zo*
CHIUSO

address *eendee-reet-so*
INDIRIZZO

here *kwee*
QUI

there *lar*
LÀ

HOW MUCH IS (THAT)? *kwan-toh coss-ta*
QUANTO COSTA?

this *kwess-toh*
QUESTO

these *kwess-tee*
QUESTI

at	by	for	from	into	to	yet
al **AL**	*pair* **PER**	*pair* **PER**	*dah* **DA**	*een* **IN**	*an* **A**	*non an-cor-ra* **NON ANCORA**

currency conversion table: 50A

now	*a-**dess**-o* **ADESSO**	exchange rate	*tass-o dee cam-beeyo* **TASSO DI CAMBIO**
later	*pee-yoo tar-dee* **PIÙ TARDI**	buying	*ak-weess-toh* **ACQUISTO**
		selling	*ven-deeta* **VENDITA**
before	***pree**-ma* **PRIMA**	commission	*comeesee-yo-nay* **COMMISSIONE**
after	***dor**-po* **DOPO**		
minutes	*mee-**noo**-tee* **MINUTI**	Bank card	*car-ta del-la bang-ka* **CARTA DELLA BANCA**
hours	*or-ray* **ORE**	Cashier's cheque	*as-sen-yo dee cassee-yair-ree* **ASSEGNO DI CASSIERE**
today	*od-jee* **OGGI**	Credit card	*car-ta dee cred-eetoh* **CARTA DI CREDITO**
tomorrow	*dom-mar-nee* **DOMANI**	Eurocheque card	*car-ta ah-yoo-ro-sheck* **CARTA EUROCHEQUE**
Monday	*loonay-dee* **LUNEDÌ**	Int'l money order	*val-ya eentair-natseeyo-nar-lay* **VAGLIA INTERNATIONALE**
morning	*mat-tee-no* **MATTINO**	Letter of credit	*let-tairra dee cred-eetoh* **LETTERA DI CREDITO**
afternoon	*pomair-reed-jo* **POMERIGGIO**	Letter of intro'	*let-tairra dee presentatsee-yo-nay* **LETTERA DI PRESENTAZIONE**
some	*kwal-kay* **QUALCHE**	Personal cheque	*ass-sen-yo pairson-nar-lay* **ASSEGNO PERSONALE**
cash	*con-tan-tee* **CONTANTI**	Statement	*bee-lan-cho* **BILANCIO**
notes/bills	*banko-not-tay* **BANCONOTE**	Transfer	*trasfairee-men-toh* **TRASFERIMENTO**
small change	*mon-net-ta* **MONETA**	Traveller's cheque/check	*trev-ooluz sheck* **TRAVELLER'S CHEQUE**
Dollars	*dol-lar-ree* **DOLLARI**	account	*ak-kon-toh* **ACCONTO**
Pounds	*stair-lee-nay* **STERLINE**	account number	*noo-mairo del con-toh* **NUMERO DEL CONTO**
Rands	*rand* **RAND**		
Lire	*lee-ray* **LIRE**	identification	*eedentee-feekatsee-yo-nay* **IDENTIFICAZIONE**
Francs	*frang-kee* **FRANCHI**	passport	*passa-por-toh* **PASSAPORTO**

english-speaking countries: 48B

Fill-in the relevant sections of the following table at current exchange rates to make a quick reference ready-reckoner helpful for when shopping.

Italian Lire	Your currency		Swiss Francs	Your currency
100	....		1	....
500	....		5	....
1000	....		10	....
2000	....		20	....
3000	....		30	....
4000	....		40	....
5000	....		50	....
6000	....		60	....
7000	....		70	....
8000	....		80	....
9000	....		90	....
10,000	....		100	....
20,000	....		200	....
30,000	....		300	....
40,000	....		400	....
50,000	....		500	....

SUGGESTED TIPPING RATES
for middle-grade establishments:

	Italy	Switzerland
Bellboy *per errand*	1000L	1F
Chambermaid *per week*	5000L	10F
Cloakroom attendant	500L	1F
Doorman *per taxi call*	500L	1F
Hairdresser	15%	10–15% (incl)
Porter (hotel) *per bag*	500L	1F
Porter (station/airport)	(fixed chg)	(fixed chg)
Taxi driver	15%	15% (often incl)
Tour guide *per day*	2000L	optional
Theatre & Cinema Usher	500L	none
Valet service	500L	1F
Waiter *(if no serv' chg)*	15%	15%
(if service incl)	5%	optional
Washroom attendant	300L	50ct

?	I	*ee-yo* **IO**					
	my	*eel **mee**-yo* **IL MIO**	would like	*vor-**ray**-ee* **VORREI**		Clean	*smac-**kee**-yar-ray* **SMACCHIARE**
	you	*lay-ee* **LEI**	want	*vwar-lay* **VUOLE**		Do	*far-ray* **FARE**
			do you have	*ah-vet-tay* **AVETE**		Dryclean	*poolee-**too**-ra ah sec-ko* **PULITURA A SECCO**
	not	*non* **NON**	is	*eh* **È**		Press	*stee-**rar**-ray* **STIRARE**
	no	*non* **NON**	are	*so-no* **SONO**		will be Ready	*sar-**rar** **pron**-toh* **SARÀ PRONTO**
	when	*kwan-doh* **QUANDO**	is there	*chay* **C'È**		Remove	*tol-**yair**-ray* **TOGLIERE**
	what	*koh-sa* **COSA**	can I have	*poss-o ah-**vair**-ray* **POSSO AVERE**		Repair	*reepar-**rar**-ray* **RIPARARE**
			can you	*pwoh* **PUÒ**		Stitch	*koo-**chee**-ray* **CUCIRE**
						will Take	*pren-day* **PRENDE**

what time	*kay **or**-ra* **CHE ORA**					
how long	*kwan-toh **tem**-po* **QUANTO TEMPO**		open	*a-**pair**-toh* **APERTO**		closed	*kee-**oo**-zo* **CHIUSO**
near	*vee-**chee**-no* **VICINO**	needle	*ar-go* **AGO**	grease	*oon-toh* **UNTO**
nearest	*pee-yoo vee-**chee**-no* **PIÙ VICINO**	thread	*fee-lo* **FILO**	hole	*boo-co* **BUCO**
here	*kwee* **QUI**	soap powder	*dettair-**see**-vo* **DETERSIVO**	stain	*mak-keeya* **MACCHIA**
there	*lar* **LÀ**	button	*bot-**toh**-nay* **BOTTONE**	boots	*stee-**var**-lay* **STIVALI**
this	*kwess-toh* **QUESTO**	clothes	*vess-**tee**-tee* **VESTITI**	sandals	*san-darlee* **SANDALI**
these	*kwess-tee* **QUESTI**	fabric	*stof-fa* **STOFFA**	shoes	*scar-pay* **SCARPE**

now	*ah-**dess**-so* **ADESSO**		HOW MUCH IS (THAT)?	*kwan-toh coss-ta* **QUANTO COSTA?**				
soon	*press-toh* **PRESTO**							
quickly	*poc-ko **tem**-po* **POCO TEMPO**	and *ay* **E**	at *al* **AL**	for *pair* **PER**	from *dah* **DA**	in *een* **IN**	on *soo* **SU**	to *ah* **A**

clothes: 37	fabrics: 38A	time: 60

?

I	*ee-yo* **IO**				
my	*eel* **mee**-*yo* **IL MIO**				
you	*lay-ee* **LEI**				
your	*eel soo-oh* **IL SUO**				
his	*eel soo-oh* **IL SUO**				
her	*la soo-ah* **LA SUA**				

would like	*vor-***ray**-*ee* **VORREI**	can I have	*poss-o ah-***vair**-*ray* **POSSO AVERE**
want	*vwar-lay* **VUOLE**	can you	*pwoh* **PUÒ**
have	*oh* **HO**	Brush	*spatso-***lar**-*ray* **SPAZZOLARE**
have	*ah* **HA**	Comb	*pettee-***nar**-*ray* **PETTINARE**
do you have	*ah-***vet**-*tay* **AVETE**	Cut	*tal-***yar**-*ray* **TAGLIARE**
is	*eh* **È**	Do	*far-ray* **FARE**
are	*so-no* **SONO**	Leave it	*lo* **lar**-*shee* **LO LASCI**
is there	*chay* **C'È**	Like it	*pee-***yar**-*chay* **MI PIACE**
		Make	*far-ray* **FARE**

not	*non* **NON**			
no	*non* **NON**			

which	*kwar-lay* **QUALE**		
where	*doh-vay* **DOVE**	nearest	*pee-***yoo** *vee-***chee**-*no* **PIÙ VICINO**
when	*kwan-doh* **QUANDO**	hairdresser	*parookee-***yair**-*ra* **PARRUCCHIERE**
what	*koh-sa* **COSA**	beauty salon	*eestee-***too**-*toh dee bel-***let**-*sa* **ISTITUTO DI BELLEZZA**
		open	*a-***pair**-*toh* **APERTO**
what time	*kay or-ra* **CHE ORA**	closed	*kee-***oo**-*zo* **CHIUSO**
		appointment	*apoonta-***mairn**-*toh* **APPUNTAMENTO**
how long	*kwan-toh tem-po* **QUANTO TEMPO**	name	*no-may* **NOME**
how much	*kwan-toh* **QUANTO**	THAT'S FINE	*va bay-nay* **VA BENE**
		HOW MUCH IS (THAT)?	*kwan-toh coss-ta* **QUANTO COSTA?**
near	*vee-***chee**-*no* **VICINO**		
here	*kwee* **QUI**		
this	*kwess-toh* **QUESTO**		

	and	at	from	in	off	on	to
	ay **E**	*al* **AL**	*dah* **DA**	*een* **IN**	*dah* **DA**	*soo* **SU**	*ah* **A**

family relations: 26　　　money & tipping: 50A　　　time: 60

too	*trop-po* **TROPPO**	Haircut	*tal-yo dee ka-pel-lee* **TAGLIO DI CAPELLI**
a little	*oon poo* **UN PÒ**	Trim	*spoonta-tee-na* **SPUNTATINA**
plenty	*mol-toh* **MOLTO**	Blowdry	*ashoo-gar-ray col fon* **ASCIUGARE COL FON**
enough	*abbass-tant-sa* **ABBASTANZA**	Manicure	*manee-koor* **MANICURE**
more	*pee-yoo* **PIÙ**	Perm	*pairma-nen-tay* **PERMANENTE**
less	*may-no* **MENO**	Rinse	*ka-shay* **CACHET**
long	*loong-go* **LUNGO**	Set	*may-sa een pee-yay-ga* **MESSA IN PIEGA**
short	*cor-toh* **CORTO**	Shampoo	*sham-poh* **SHAMPO**
hot	*cal-doh* **CALDO**	Shave	*raza-too-ra* **RASATURA**
cold	*fray-doh* **FREDDO**	Touch-up	*reetoh-ka-tee-na* **RITOCCATINA**

same	*stess-so* **STESSO**	new	*noo-woh-vo* **NUOVO**
style	*stee-lay* **STILE**	colour	*col-lor-ray* **COLORE**
front	*fron-tay* **FRONTE**	back	*dee-yet-ro* **DIETRO**
top	*sop-ra* **SOPRA**	sides	*ayee lar-tee* **AI LATI**
black	*nair-ro* **NERO**	blond	*bee-yon-doh* **BIONDO**
brunette	*broo-no* **BRUNO**	auburn	*cass-tar-no* **CASTANO**
lighter	*pee-yoo kee-yar-ro* **PIÙ CHIARO**		
darker	*pee-yoo skoo-roh* **PIÙ SCURO**		
colour chart	*ta-bel-la day col-lor-ray* **TABELLA DEI COLORI**		

Layered	*ah strar-tee* **A STRATI**		
Shaped	*stee-lay* **STILE**		
Streaked	mesh **MESH**		
Curly	*ree-cha* **RICCIA**		
Fluffy	*cotto-nar-ta* **COTONATA**		
Fringe	*fran-jee-ya* **FRANGIA**		
Ringlets	*ree-cho-lee* **RICCIOLI**		
Wavy	*ondoo-lar-tee* **ONDULATI**		

Beard	*bar-ba* **BARBA**
Hair	*cap-pel-lee* **CAPELLI**
Moustache	*bar-fee* **BAFFI**
Sideboards Sideburns	*bar-zet-tay* **BASETTE**

Conditioner	*condeetseeyona-tor-ray* **CONDIZIONATORE**		
Cream	*cray-ma* **CREMA**	Lacquer	*lac-ka* **LACCA**
Oil	*ol-yo* **OLIO**	Tonic	*lotsee-yo-nay* **LOZIONE**

colours/colori: 38A

?

I	*ee-yo* **IO**	
my	*eel mee-yo* **IL MIO**	
you	*lay-ee* **LEI**	
your	*eel soo-oh* **IL SUO**	
he	*lwee* **LUI**	
she	*lay-ee* **LEI**	
his	*eel soo-oh* **IL SUO**	
her	*lah soo-ah* **LA SUA**	
it	*ay-so* **ESSO**	
not	*non* **NON**	
no	*non* **NON**	

would like	*vor-ray-ee* **VORREI**		is there	*chay* **C'È**
want	*vwar-lay* **VUOLE**		Check	*con-tro-lo* **CONTROLLO**
have	*oh* **HO**		Come back	*reetor-nar-ray* **RITORNARE**
have	*ah* **HA**		Fix	*coo-rar-ray* **CURARE**
is	*eh* **È**		Hurts	*fah mar-lay* **FA MALE**
are	*so-no* **SONO**		Need	*ah bee-zon-yo dee* **HA BISOGNO DI**
can I	*poss-o* **POSSO**		Pay	*pa-gar-ray* **PAGARE**
can I have	*poss-o ah-vair-ray* **POSSO AVERE**		to See	*ved-dair-ray* **VEDERE**
can you	*pwoh* **PUÒ**		Send	*man-dar-ray* **MANDARE**
			will Take	*pren-day* **PRENDE**

		very	*mol-toh* **MOLTO**	nearest	*pee-yoo vee-chee-no* **PIÙ VICINO**
which	*kwar-lay* **QUALE**	soon	*press-toh* **PRESTO**		
where	*doh-vay* **DOVE**	urgently	*oorjenta-men-tay* **URGENTEMENTE**	appointment	*appoonta-men-toh* **APPUNTAMENTO**
when	*kwan-doh* **QUANDO**	earlier	*pee-yoo press-toh* **PIÙ PRESTO**		
		now	*ah-dess-o* **ADESSO**	open	*a-pair-toh* **APERTO**
what time	*kay or-ra* **CHE ORA**	later	*pee-yoo tar-dee* **PIÙ TARDI**	closed	*kee-oo-zo* **CHIUSO**

how long	*kwan-toh tem-po* **QUANTO TEMPO**	HOW MUCH WILL IT COST!	*kwan-toh costair-ra* **QUANTO COSTERÀ**
how much	*kwan-toh* **QUANTO**	HOW MUCH IS (THAT)?	*kwan-toh coss-ta* **QUANTO COSTA?**

near	*vee-chee-no* **VICINO**
here	kwee **QUI**

	at	for	from	in	on	to	with
	al **AL**	*pair* **PER**	*dah* **DA**	*dee* **DI**	*soo* **SU**	*ah* **A**	*con* **CON**

more medical questions/altre domande mediche: 53

English	Pronunciation / Italian		English	Pronunciation / Italian
this (one)	kwess-toh **QUESTO**		Crown	cor-ro-na **CORONA**
somewhere	een kwal-kay par-tay **IN QUALCHE PARTE**		Gum	jen-jee-va **GENGIVA**
here	kwee **QUI**		Jaw	ma-shel-la **MASCELLA**
			Tooth	den-tay **DENTE**
very	mol-toh **MOLTO**		Dentures	dentee-yair-ra **DENTIERA**
slight	led-jair-ro **LEGGERO**			
severe	grar-vay **GRAVE**			
abscess	ah-shess-o **ASCESSO**		Bleeding	sang-gweena **SANGUINA**
toothache	mal dee den-tee **MAL DI DENTI**		Broken	rot-toh **ROTTO**
			Come out	cad-doo-toh **CADUTO**
periodic	pairree-yod-deeko **PERIODICO**		Decayed	carree-yar-toh **CARIATO**
constant	coss-tan-tay **COSTANTE**		Infected	conta-jar-toh **CONTAGIATO**
throbbing	pool-san-tay **PULSANTE**		Loose	dondoh-larn-tay **DONDOLANTE**
pain	dol-lor-ray **DOLORE**		Painful	dollor-ro-so **DOLOROSO**
hot & cold	cal-doh ay fray-doh **CALDO E FREDDO**		Sensitive	sensee-tee-vo **SENSITIVO**
			Sore	eenfeeya-mar-ta **INFIAMMATA**
necessary	netchay-sar-reeyo **NECESSARIO**			
temporary	provee-zor-reeyo **PROVVISORIO**			
			Allergic	al-lair-jeeko **ALLERGICO**
name	no-may **NOME**		Antibiotic	anteebee-yot-teeko **ANTIBIOTICO**
address	eendee-reet-so **INDIRIZZO**		Extraction	estratsee-yo-nay **ESTRAZIONE**
here/at home	kwee/ah cass-sa **QUI A CASA**		Filling	otoo-ratsee-yo-nay **OTTURAZIONE**
insurance	asseekoo-ratsee-yo-nay **ASSICURAZIONE**		Gas	gas **GAS**
receipt	reechay-voo-ta **RICEVUTA**		Injection	eenyetsee-yo-nay **INIEZIONE**

family relations/parenti: 26   payment/pagamento: 55B

?

I	*ee-yo* **IO**	want	*vol-yo* **VOGLIO**	Check *control-lar-ray* **CONTROLLARE**
me	*may* **ME**	want	*vwar-lay* **VOULE**	Come back *reetor-nar-ray* **RITORNARE**
my	*eel mee-yo* **IL MIO**			Cough *toss-see-ray* **TOSSIRE**
you	*lay-ee* **LEI**	have	*oh* **HO**	Drink *bair-ray* **BERE**
your	*eel soo-oh* **IL SUO**	have	*ah* **HA**	Eat *man-jar-ray* **MANGIARE**
he	*lwee* **LUI**	do you have	*ah-vet-tay* **AVETE**	Feel(s) *sen-teer-see* **SENTIRSI**
she	*lay-ee* **LEI**			Feel ill *mee sen-toh mar-lay* **MI SENTO MALE**
his	*eel soo-oh* **IL SUO**	am	*so-no* **SONO**	Give *dar-ray* **DARE**
her	*la soo-ah* **LA SUA**	is	*eh* **È**	Go *an-dar-ray* **ANDARE**
it	*ay-so* **ESSO**	are	*so-no* **SONO**	Hear *oo-dee-ray* **UDIRE**
they	*ess-ee* **ESSI**			Hurts *mee fah mar-lay* **MI FA MALE**
		is there	*chay* **C'È**	Move *mwo-vair-ray* **MUOVERE**
not	*non* **NON**	can I	*poss-o* **POSSO**	Need(s) *oh bee-son-yo dee* **HO BISOGNO DI**
no	*non* **NON**	can I have	*poss-o ah-vair-ray* **POSSO AVERE**	Open *ap-pree-ray* **APRIRE**
		I cannot	*non poss-o* **NON POSSO**	Rest *reepo-sar-see* **RIPOSARSI**
which	*kwar-lay* **QUALE**	can you	*pwoh* **PUÒ**	See *ved-dair-ray* **VEDERE**
where	*doh-vay* **DOVE**			Sleep *dor-mee-ray* **DORMIRE**
when	*kwan-doh* **QUANDO**	I must	*day-vo* **DEVO**	Stay *res-tar-ray* **RESTARE**
what time	*kay or-ra* **CHE ORA**	you must	*day-vay* **DEVE**	Swallow *eeng-gheeyo-tee-ray* **INGHIOTTIRE**
how	*koh-may* **COME**			Take *pren-dair-ray* **PRENDERE**
how many	*kwan-tee* **QUANTI**	Breathe	*respee-rar-ray* **RESPIRARE**	
how much	*kwan-toh* **QUANTO**	(in/out)	*(den-tro / fwor-ree)* **(DENTRO FUORI)**	Vomit *vommee-tar-ray* **VOMITARE**
how long	*kwan-toh tem-po* **QUANTO TEMPO**			

Point out the following paragraph to the person you are talking to. It explains how to use this section of the Phrasemaker.

Indicare le parole per formulare frasi semplici. Non preoccuparsi per la grammatica. Riferisi alle altre pagine (elencate a fondo pagina) per altre descrizioni di carattere medico. È d'aiuto usare segni.

very	*mol-toh* **MOLTO**	temperature	*tempaira-too-ra* **TEMPERATURA**	
severe	*grar-vay* **GRAVE**	blood pressure	*pressee-yo-nay del sang-gway* **PRESSIONE DEL SANGUE**	
slight	*led-jair-ro* **LEGGERO**	hot	*cal-doh* **CALDO**	cold *fray-doh* **FREDDO**
pain	*dol-lor-ray* **DOLORE**	high	*al-ta* **ALTA**	low *bass-ah* **BASSA**
here	*kwee* **QUI**			

		left	*see-neess-tro* **SINISTRO**	
frequent	*fray-kwen-tay* **FREQUENTE**	right	*dess-tro* **DESTRO**	
sudden	*eempro-vee-zo* **IMPROVVISO**	side	*lar-toh* **LATO**	

every	*on-yee* **OGNI**	more	*pee-yoo* **PIÙ**	
hours	*or-ray* **ORE**	less	*mayno* **MENO**	
days	*jor-nee* **GIORNI**			

		start	*ee-neet-seeyo* **INIZIO**	
now	*a-dess-o* **ADESSO**	stop	*fee-nay* **FINE**	
later	*pee-yoo tar-dee* **PIÙ TARDI**	first time	*pree-ma vol-ta* **PRIMA VOLTA**	
before	*pree-ma* **PRIMA**	long time	*tan-toh tem-po* **TANTO TEMPO**	
after	*dor-po* **DOPO**	recently	*retchentay-men-tay* **RECENTEMENTE**	

family	*fam-meel-ya* **FAMIGLIA**	at	for	from	in	on	to	with
history of	*stor-reeya dee* **STORIA DI**	*al* **AL**	*pair* **PER**	*dah* **DA**	*een* **IN**	*soo* **SU**	*ah* **A**	*con* **CON**

family relations parenti :26	ailments malattie :56A	diagnoses/medications diagnosi / cura :56B	payment pagamento :55B

SYMPTOMS	*seen-toh-mee* **SINTOMI**	Aching	*dol-lair-ray* **DOLERE**
Burning feeling	*sen-so dee broocheeya-too-ra* **SENSO BRUCIATURA**	Bleeding	*sang-gweena* **SANGUINA**
(a) Cold	*raffred-dor-ray* **RAFFREDDORE**	Blocked	*bloc-kar-toh* **BLOCCATO**
Constipation	*costeepatsee-yo-nay* **COSTIPAZIONE**	Depressed	*day-press-o* **DEPRESSO**
Convulsions	*convool-see-yo-nee* **CONVULSIONI**	Dizzy	*stor-dee-toh* **STORDITO**
(a) Cough	*toss-ay* **TOSSE**	Faint	*day-boh-lay* **DEBOLE**
Cramps	*crarm-pee* **CRAMPI**	Feverish	*febreechee-tan-tay* **FEBBRICITANTE**
Diarrhea	*deeyar-ray-ah* **DIARREA**	Hurting	*dol-lair-ray* **DOLERE**
Ear ache	*mal dor-reck-eeyo* **MAL D'ORECCHIO**	Ill	*mal-lar-toh* **MALATO**
Hay fever	*feb-bray da fee-yay-no* **FEBBRE DA FIENO**	Infected	*eenfet-tar-toh* **INFETTATO**
Headache	*mal dee tess-ta* **MAL DI TESTA**	Injured	*fair-ree-ta* **FERITA**
Indigestion	*eendeejestee-yo-nay* **INDIGESTIONE**	Itchy	*proo-ree-toh* **PRURITO**
Migraine	*emee-krar-neeya* **EMICRANIA**	Numb	*eentorpee-dee-toh* **INTORPIDITO**
Morning sickness	*now-saya all mat-tee-no* **NAUSEA AL MATTINO**	Oozing	*soopoo-rartsee-yo-nay* **SUPPURAZIONE**
Nausea	*now-saya* **NAUSEA**	Painful	*dollor-ro-so* **DOLOROSO**
Pain	*dol-lor-ray* **DOLORE**	Paralysed	*paraleet-sar-toh* **PARALIZZATO**
Palpitations	*parlpee-tatsee-yo-nay* **PALPITAZIONE**	Running	*poo-roo-len-tay* **PURULENTE**
Sore throat	*mal dee go-la* **MAL DI GOLA**	Shaky	*trem-man-tay* **TREMANTE**
Short of breath	*cor-toh dee fee-yartoh* **CORTO DI FIATO**	Shivery	*rabreevee-dee-ray* **RABBRIVIDIRE**
Stomach ache	*mal dee stom-marco* **MAL DI STOMACO**	Sneezing	*stair-noo-toh* **STERNUTO**
Sunburn	*scotta-too-ra sol-lar-ray* **SCOTTATURA SOLARE**	Stiff	*ree-jee-doh* **RIGIDO**
(a) Temperature	*la feb-bray* **LA FEBBRE**	Tired	*starn-co* **STANCO**
Travel sickness	*mal dee vee-yar-jo* **MAL DI VIAGGIO**	Weak	*day-vollay* **DEBOLE**

body parts: 55   **ailments/diagnosis: 56**

WOUNDS	*fair-ree-tay* **FERITE**	BODY FLUIDS	*floo-wee-dee del corpo* **FLUIDI DEL CORPO**
Bite	*mor-so* **MORSO**	Blood	*sang-gway* **SANGUE**
Blister	*vair-shee-ka* **VESCICA**	Blood group	*groo-po sang-gween-yo* **GRUPPO SANGUIGNO**
Boil	*for-roong-collo* **FORUNCOLO**	Menses	*mestroo-atsee-yo-nee* **MESTRUAZIONE**
Bruise	*contoosee-yo-nay* **CONTUSIONE**	Phlegm	*flem-mah* **FLEMMA**
Burn	*scotta-too-ra* **SCOTTATURA**	Pus	*pooss* **PUS**
Cut	*tar-lyo* **TAGLIO**	Saliva	*sal-lee-va* **SALIVA**
Infection	*eenfetsee-yo-nay* **INFEZIONE**	Stools	*fet-chee* **FECI**
Rash	*ayzan-tay-ma* **ESANTEMA**	Urine	*oo-ree-na* **URINA**
Sting	*poon-too-ra* **PUNTURA**	Vomit	*vom-meetoh* **VOMITO**
Sunburn	*scotta-too-ra da so-lay* **SCOTTATURA DA SOLE**		
Swelling	*toomay-fatsee-yo-nay* **TUMEFAZIONE**	light	*kee-yar-ro* **CHIARO**
		dark	*skoo-ro* **SCURO**
		black	*nair-ro* **NERO**
DAMAGE	*dar-no* **DANNO**	green	*vair-day* **VERDE**
Burnt	*oosteeyo-nar-toh* **USTIONATO**	red	*ross-o* **ROSSO**
Bruised	*con-too-zo* **CONTUSO**	yellow	*jar-lo* **GIALLO**
Broken	*rot-toh* **ROTTO**		
Cut	*tal-yar-toh* **TAGLIATO**	slight	*led-jair-ro* **LEGGERO**
Dislocated	*deesloc-kar-toh* **DISLOCATO**	severe	*for-tay* **FORTE**
Grazed	*scal-fee-toh* **SCALFITO**	left	*see-neess-tro* **SINISTRO**
Ruptured	*air-nee-ya* **ERNIA**	right	*dess-tro* **DESTRO**
Sprained	*slog-gar-toh* **SLOGATO**	side	*lar-toh* **LATO**
Torn	*strap-par-toh* **STRAPPATO**	here	*kwee* **QUI**

parti del corpo: 55   malattie/diagnosi: 56

BODY PARTS *par*-tee del *cor*-po
PARTI DEL CORPO

Ankle	ka-*veel*-ya **CAVIGLIA**		Forehead	*fron*-tay **FRONTE**
Anus	*ar*-no **ANO**		Gland	*ghee*-ando-la **GHIANDOLA**
Appendix	appen-*dee*-chay **APPENDICE**		Hair	cap-*pel*-lee **CAPELLI**
Arm	*brar*-cho **BRACCIO**		Hand	*mar*-no **MANO**
Artery	ar-*tair*-reeya **ARTERIA**		Head	*tess*-tah **TESTA**
Baby	*beem*-bo **BIMBO**		Heart	*kwor*-ray **CUORE**
Back	skee-*yay*-na **SCHIENA**		Heel	tal-*lo*-nay **TALLONE**
Bladder	vesh-*ee*-ka oo-ree-*nar*-reeya **VESCICA URINARIA**		Hip	*ang*-ka **ANCA**
Bone	*oss*-so **OSSO**		Intestines	eentes-*tee*-nee **INTESTINI**
Bowels	boo-*del*-la **BUDELLA**		Jaw	ma-*shel*-la **MASCELLA**
Breast	*pet*-toh **PETTO**		Joint	joon-*too*-ra **GIUNTURA**
Cheek	*gwan*-cha **GUANCIA**		Kidney	*ren*-nay **RENE**
Chest	tor-*rat*-chay **TORACE**		Knee	jee-*noc*-keeyo **GINOCCHIO**
Chin	*mayn*-toh **MENTO**		Leg	*gam*-ba **GAMBA**
Collarbone	cla-*vee*-co-la **CLAVICOLA**		Ligament	legga-*men*-toh **LEGAMENTO**
Ear	or-*ray*-keeyo **ORECCHIO**		Lip	*lab*-bro **LABBRO**
Elbow	*gom*-meetoh **GOMITO**		Liver	*feg*-gartoh **FEGATO**
Eye	*ock*-keeyo **OCCHIO**		Lung	pol-*mo*-nay **POLMONE**
Eyes	*ock*-kee **OCCHI**		Lungs	pol-*mo*-nee **POLMONI**
Face	*vee*-zo **VISO**		Mouth	*boc*-ka **BOCCA**
Finger	*dee*-toh del-la *mar*-no **DITO DELLA MANO**		Muscle	*moos*-co-lo **MUSCOLO**
Foot	pee-*yay*-day **PIEDE**		Nail	*oong*-gheeya **UNGHIA**

symptoms: 54A   wounds/damage/body fluids: 54B   ailments: 56

Neck	*col-lo*	**COLLO**
Nerve	*nair-vo*	**NERVO**
Nerv' system	*sees-**tem**-ma nair-vo-so*	**SISTEMA NERVOSO**
Nose	*nar-zo*	**NASO**
Penis	*pen-nay*	**PENE**
Rib	*coss-toh-la*	**COSTOLA**
Shoulder	*spar-la*	**SPALLA**
Skin	*pel-lay*	**PELLE**
Skull	*crar-neeyo*	**CRANIO**
Spine	*spee-na dor-sar-lay*	**SPINA DORSALE**
Stomach	*stom-maco*	**STOMACO**
Testes	*tess-tee-co-lee*	**TESTICOLI**
Tendon	*ten-deenay*	**TENDINE**
Thigh	*co-sha*	**COSCIA**
Throat	*go-la*	**GOLA**
Thumb	*pol-leechay*	**POLLICE**
Toe	*dee-toh del pee-yay-day*	**DITO DEL PIEDE**
Tongue	*leeng-gwa*	**LINGUA**
Tonsils	*ton-see-lay*	**TONSILLE**
Vagina	*var-jee-na*	**VAGINA**
Vein	*vay-na*	**VENA**
Wrist	*pol-so*	**POLSO**

slight	*led-jair-ro*	**LEGGERO**
severe	*for-tay*	**FORTE**
pain	*dol-lor-ray*	**DOLORE**
left	*see-neess-tro*	**SINISTRO**
right	*dess-tro*	**DESTRO**
side	*lar-toh*	**LATO**
here	*kwee*	**QUI**

PAYMENT — *pagga-**men**-toh* **PAGAMENTO**

how much will cost?	*kwan-toh costair-ra*	**QUANTO COSTERÀ?**
how much is bill/check?	*kwan-toh eh eel con-toh*	**QUANTO È IL CONTO?**
pay now	*par-go or-ra*	**PAGO ORA**
pay later	*par-go dor-po*	**PAGO DOPO**
send bill/check	*man-dar-ray eel con-toh*	**MANDARE IL CONTO**
name	*no-may*	**NOME**
address	*eendee-reet-so*	**INDIRIZZO**
here	*kwee*	**QUI**
home	*cass-a*	**CASA**
identification	*eedentee-feekatsee-yo-nay*	**IDENTIFICAZIONE**
insurance	*asseekoo-ratsee-yo-nay*	**ASSICURAZIONE**
receipt	*reechay-voo-ta*	**RICEVUTA**

sintomi: 54A   ferite/danno/fluidi del corpo: 54B   malattie: 56

AILMENTS	*malla-tee-yay* **MALATTIE**	Heart attack	*at-tac-ko car-dee-yarco* **ATTACCO CARDIACO**
Abscess	*ah-shess-so* **ASCESSO**	Hepatitis	*eppar-tee-tay* **EPATITE**
Anemia	*annay-mee-ya* **ANEMIA**	Herpes	*air-pettay* **ERPETE**
Appendicitis	*appendee-chee-tay* **APPENDICITE**	Hernia	*air-neeya* **ERNIA**
Arthritis	*ar-tree-tay* **ARTRITE**	(High/low) blood pressure	*(al-ta/ bass-sa) pressee-yo-nay* **(ALTA BASSA) PRESSIONE**
Asthma	*az-ma* **ASMA**	Infection	*eenfetsee-yo-nay* **INFEZIONE**
Blood clot	*groo-mo dee sang-gway* **GRUMO DI SANGUE**	Inflammation of	*eenfeeya-matsee-yo-nay ah* **INFIAMMAZIONE A**
Bronchitis	*bron-kee-tay* **BRONCHITE**	Influenza	*eenfloo-went-sah* **INFLUENZA**
Cancer	*can-cro* **CANCRO**	Kidney stones	*carl-colee ay ray-nee* **CALCOLI AI RENI**
Cardiac cond	*mal dee kwor-ray* **MAL DI CUORE**	Leukemia	*layoochay-mee-ya* **LEUCEMIA**
(a) Cold	*raffred-dor-ray* **RAFFREDDORE**	Morning sickness	*now-saya al mat-tee-no* **NAUSEA AL MATTINO**
Colitis	*col-lee-tay* **COLITE**	Nervous tension	*tensee-yo-nay nair-voh-sah* **TENSIONE NERVOSA**
Congestion	*conjestee-yo-nay* **CONGESTIONE**	Over-tired	*trop-po stan-co* **TROPPO STANCO**
Diabetes	*deeya-bet-tay* **DIABETE**	Parasites	*para-see-tee* **PARASSITI**
Drug overdose	*doss-say etchess-see-va dee drog-ga* **DOSE ECCESSIVA DI DROGA**	Pneumonia	*polmon-nee-tay* **POLMONITE**
Dysentry	*deesentair-ree-ya* **DISSENTERIA**	Pulled muscle	*strar-po moosco-lar-ray* **STRAPPO MUSCOLARE**
Epilepsy	*epeeless-ee-ya* **EPILESSIA**	Rheumatism	*rayoomar-teez-mee* **REUMATISMI**
Fever	*feb-bray* **FEBBRE**	Slipped disc	*air-neeya del deess-ko* **ERNIA DEL DISCO**
Food poisoning	*eentossee-car-toh dal chee-bo* **INTOSSICATO DAL CIBO**	Stroke	*col-po appop-plet-teeko* **COLPO APOPLETTICO**
Gall stones	*carl-colee beelee-yar-ree* **CALCOLI BILIARI**	Sunstroke	*col-po dee sol-lay* **COLPO DI SOLE**
Haemorrhoids	*emmor-ro-eedee* **EMORROIDI**	Tonsilitis	*tonsee-lee-tay* **TONSILLITE**
Hay fever	*feb-bray dah fee-yay-no* **FEBBRE DA FIENO**	Ulcer	*ool-chair-ra* **ULCERA**
		VD	*malla-tee-yay ven-nair-ree* **MALATTIE VENEREE**

symptoms: 54A   wounds/damage/body fluids: 54B   body parts: 55

DIAGNOSIS	*dee-yan-oh-see* **DIAGNOSI**	MEDICINES	*medee-chee-nay* **MEDICINE**
probably	*probba-beel-men-tay* **PROBABILMENTE**	Capsules	*com-press-ay* **COMPRESSE**
(not) serious	*(non) grar-vay* **(NON) GRAVE**	Cream	*cray-ma* **CREMA**
emergency	*eemair-jent-sa* **EMERGENZA**	Drops	*got-chay* **GOCCE**
		Lotion	*lo-tsee-yo-nay* **LOZIONE**
Blood pressure	*pressee-yo-nay del sang-gway* **PRESSIONE DEL SANGUE**	Powder	*pol-vair-ray* **POLVERE**
Check-up	*con-troh-lo* **CONTROLLO**	Tablets	*pas-tee-leeyay* **PASTIGLIE**
Operation	*oppair-ratsee-yo-nay* **OPERAZIONE**	Tonic	*tonneko* **TONICO**
Specimen	*cam-pee-yo-nay* **CAMPIONE**		
Temperature	*tempairra-too-ra* **TEMPERATURA**	MEDICAL INSTRUCTIONS	*eestrootsee-yo-nee med-eekay* **ISTRUZIONI MEDICHE**
X-ray	*rar-dee-yo-grar-fee-ya* **RADIOGRAFIA**	dosage	*doss-say* **DOSE**
		teaspoonfuls	*kookeeya-ee-no dah tay pee-yay-no* **CUCCHIAINO DA TÈ PIENO**
in bed	*ah let-toh* **A LETTO**	times daily	*vol-tay al jorno* **VOLTE AL GIORNO**
hospital	*osped-dar-lay* **OSPEDALE**	swallow whole	*eeng-gheeyo-tee-ray een-tair-ray* **INGHIOTTIRE INTERE**
		every....hours	*on-yee....or-ray* **OGNI.... ORE**
Allergic	*al-lair-jeeco* **ALLERGICO**	before	*pree-ma* **PRIMA** after *dor-po* **DOPO**
Antibiotic	*anteebee-yot-toeeko* **ANTIBIOTICO**	between	*frah* **FRA** with *con* **CON**
Injection	*eenyetsee-yo-nay* **INIEZIONE**		
Insulin	*eensoo-leena* **INSULINA**	meals	*pas-tee* **PASTI**
Prescription	*ree-chet-ta* **RICETTA**	water	*ak-wa* **ACQUA**
Pain reliever	*carl-man-tay* **CALMANTE**	in morning	*al mat-tee-no* **AL MATTINO**
Sedative	*sedda-tee-vo* **SEDATIVO**	at night	*alla not-tay* **ALLA NOTTE**
Sleeping pills	*son-nee-fairree* **SONNIFERI**	using toilet	*an-dar-ray alla toy-let-tay* **ANDARE ALLA TOILETTE**

sintomi: 54A   ferite/danno/fluido del corpo: 54B   parte del corpo: 55

?

I	*ee-yo*	**IO**
me	*may*	**ME**
my	*eel mee-yo*	**IL MIO**
you	*lay-ee*	**LEI**
your	*eel soo-oh*	**IL SUO**
not	*non*	**NON**
no	*non*	**NON**
which	*kwar-lay*	**QUALE**
where	*doh-vay*	**DOVE**
when	*kwan-doh*	**QUANDO**
what	*koh-sa*	**COSA**
what time	*kay or-ra*	**CHE ORA**
how long	*kwan-toh tempo*	**QUANTO TEMPO**
how many	*kwan-tee*	**QUANTI**
how much	*kwan-toh*	**QUANTO**

want	*vol-yo*	**VOGLIO**
you want	*vwar-lay*	**VUOLE**
have	*oh*	**HO**
have	*ah*	**HA**
am	*so-no*	**SONO**
is	*eh*	**È**
are	*so-no*	**SONO**
can I	*poss-o*	**POSSO**
can I have	*poss-o ah-vair-ray*	**POSSO AVERE**
can you	*pwoh*	**PUÒ**

Check	*control-lar-ray*	**CONTROLLARE**
Drink	*bair-ray*	**BERE**
Eat	*man-jay-ray*	**MANGIARE**
Feel	*sen-tee-ray*	**SENTIRE**
Help me	*mee ah-yoo-tee*	**MI AIUTI**
Give me	*mee dee-ya*	**MI DIA**
Go	*an-dar-ray*	**ANDARE**
See	*ved-dair-ray*	**VEDERE**
Sleep	*dor-mee-ray*	**DORMIRE**
Stay	*ress-tar-ray*	**RESTARE**
Take	*pren-dair-ray*	**PRENDERE**

SAMPLES	*campee-yo-nee*	**CAMPIONI**	PEOPLE	*gen-tay*	**GENTE**
blood	*sang-gway*	**SANGUE**	doctor	*med-eeco*	**MEDICO**
blood grp	*groo-po sang-gween-yo*	**GRUPPO SANGUIGNO**	nurse	*eenfairmee-yair-ra*	**INFERMIERA**
saliva	*sa-lee-va*	**SALIVA**	visitor	*veezeeta-tor-ray*	**VISITATORE**
stools	*fet-chee*	**FECI**	physiotherapist	*feezeeyo-taira-peess-ta*	**FISIOTERAPISTA**
urine	*oo-ree-na*	**URINA**	specialist	*spetchal-leess-ta*	**SPECIALISTA**

near	*vee-chee-no*	**VICINO**
here	*kwee*	**QUI**
this	*kwess-toh*	**QUESTO**

	any	for	from	in	on	to	with
	del	*pair*	*dah*	*een*	*soo*	*ah*	*con*
	DEL	**PER**	**DA**	**IN**	**SU**	**A**	**CON**

family relations: 26   doctor: 53   payment: 55B   time: 60

faint	**day**-bollay **DEBOLE**
nauseous	**now**-saya **NAUSEA**
pain	dol-**lor**-ray **DOLORE**
shaky	trem-**man**-tay **TREMANTE**
hot	**cal**-doh **CALDO**
cold	**fray**-doh **FREDDO**

EQUIPMENT	ekwee-parja-**men**-toh **EQUIPAGGIAMENTO**
Bed	**let**-toh **LETTO**
Bed pan	pa-**del**-la dah **let**-toh **PADELLA DA LETTO**
Headphones	**koo**-feeyay **CUFFIE**
Meal tray	vass-**so**-eeyo **VASSOIO**
Pyjamas	pee-**jar**-ma **PIGIAMA**
Respirator	respee-rat-**tor**-ray **RESPIRATORE**
Telephone	tel-**lef**-onno **TELEFONO**
Urine bottle	bo-**teel**-ya oo-**ree**-na **BOTTIGLIA URINA**

ROOMS	**cam**-mair-ray **CAMERE**
Day room	sod-**jor**-no **SOGGIORNO**
Dining room	**sar**-la dah **prant**-so **SALA DA PRANZO**
Operating theatre	**sar**-la opaira-**tor**-reeya **SALA OPERATORIA**
Toilet	toi-**let**-tay **TOILETTE**
Ward	cor-**see**-ya **CORSIA**

TREATMENTS	**koo**-ra **CURA**
Allergy	allair-**jee**-ya **ALLERGIA**
Bath	**ban**-yo **BAGNO**
Examination	ez-**zar**-may **ESAME**
Exercise	essair-**cheet**-seeyo **ESERCIZIO**
General anaesthetic	anestay-**see**-ya jennair-**rar**-lay **ANESTESIA GENERALE**
Injection	eenyetsee-**yo**-nay **INIEZIONE**
Intensive care	**koo**-ra eenten-**see**-va **CURA INTENSIVA**
Intravenous	eentravay-**no**-so **INTRAVENOSO**
Local anaesthetic	anestay-**see**-ya lo-**car**-lay **ANESTESIA LOCALE**
Medicine	medee-**chee**-na **MEDICINA**
Operation	opair-ratsee-**yo**-nay **OPERAZIONE**
Oxygen	ossee-**jair**-no **OSSIGENO**
Pain reliever	carl-**man**-tay **CALMANTE**
Physical therapy	feezeeyo-tairra-**pee**-ya **FISIOTERAPIA**
Plaster cast	eenjessa-**too**-ra **INGESSATURA**
Prescription	ree-**chet**-tah **RICETTA**
Sedative	sedda-**tee**-vo **SEDATIVO**
Stitches	**poon**-tee **PUNTI**
Temperature	tempairra-**too**-ra **TEMPERATURA**
Transfusion	trasfoozee-**yo**-nay **TRASFUSIONE**
X-ray	**rar**-deeyo-grar-**fee**-ya **RADIOGRAFIA**

parenti: 26   medico: 53   paggamento: 55B   tempo: 60

ABBREVIATIONS

a	**ARRIVO**	arrival
a.C	**AVANTI CRISTO**	B.C.
A.C.I	**AUTOMOBILE CLUB D'ITALIA**	Automobile Assn of Italy
A.C.S	**AUTOMOBILE CLUB SVIZZERO**	Automobile Assn of Switzerland
a.D	**ANNO DOMINI**	A.D
alt	**ALTITUDE**	altitude
ca	**CIRCA**	about
C.I.T	**COMPAGNIA ITALIANA TURISMO**	Italian travel agency
C.so	**CORSO**	avenue
d.C	**DOPO CRISTO**	A.D
E.N.I.T	**ENTE NAZIONALE INDUSTRIE TURISTICHE**	Italian national tourist organisation
F.F.S	**FERROVIE FEDERALI SVIZZERE**	Swiss federal railway
F.S	**FERROVIE DELLO STATO**	Italian railway
I.V.A	**IMPOSTA SUL VALORE AGGIUNTO**	V.A.T (sales tax)
Mil	**MILITARE**	military
p	**PARTENZA**	departure
P.T	**POSTE & TELECOMUNICAZIONI**	Post & Telecom'
P.za	**PIAZZA**	square
R.A.I	**RADIO AUDIZIONI ITALIANE**	Italian broadcasting company
Sig	**SIGNORE**	Mr
Sig.na	**SIGNORINA**	Miss
Sig.ra	**SIGNORA**	Mrs
S.I.P	**SOCIETÀ ITALIANA PER L'ESERCIZIO TELEFONICO**	Italian telephone company
s.p.a	**SOCIETÀ PER AZIONI**	Ltd., Inc., Pty Ltd.
T.C.I	**TOURING CLUB ITALIANO**	Italian touring assoc
T.C.S	**TOURING CLUB SVIZZERO**	Swiss touring assoc
V.le	**VIALE**	avenue
V.U	**VIGILI URBANI**	city police

PUBLIC HOLIDAYS

January 1	**New Year's Day**	I & S	I = Italy
January 2	" " "	S	S = Switzerland
April 25	**Liberation Day**	I	
May 1	**Labour Day**	I	
August 15	**Assumption Day**	I	
November 1	**All Saints' Day**	I	
December 8	**Immaculate Conception**	I	
December 25	**Christmas Day**	I & S	
December 26	**St Stephen's Day**	I & S	
	Easter Monday	I & S	
	Ascension Day	I & S	
	Good Friday	S	
	Whit Monday	S	

ACQUA POTABILE	Drinking water	**INFORMAZIONE**	Information
AFFITTASI	To let	**IN VENDITA**	For sale
A NOLO	To hire	**LIBERO**	Vacant
AL MARE	To the sea	**METÀ PREZZO**	Half-price
ALT	Stop	**NON CALPESTARE L'ERBA**	Don't walk on the grass
APERTO	Open	**OCCASIONI**	Bargains
ASCENSORE	Lift	**OCCUPATO**	Occupied
ATTENTI AL CANE	Beware of dog	**ORARIO**	Timetable/Opening hours
ATTRAVERSARE	Cross now	**ORARIO DI PARTENZA**	Departure times
AUTO SERVIZIO	Self-service	**ORARIO D'UFFICIO**	Office hours
AVANTI	Cross now/Come in	**PAGARE QUI**	Pay here
BARCHE A NOLEGGIO	Boats for hire	**PARTENZE**	Departures
BIBITE FREDDE	Cold drinks	**PER FAVORE ATTENDERE**	Please wait
BIGLIETTERIA	Booking office	**PIENO**	Full
CALDO	Hot	**PERICOLO**	Danger
CAMBIO	Money change	**PISCINA**	Swimming pool
CAMPEGGIO	Camping	**PRENOTATO**	Reserved
CARABINIERI	Police	**PRIVATO**	Private
CASSA	Cash desk	**PRUDENZA**	Caution
CASSIERE	Cashier	**RESA VUOTI**	Return empties
CHIUSO	Closed	**RIBASSATA**	Reduced (price)
CINTURE DI	Lifebelts	**RISERVATO**	Reserved
-SALVATAGGIO		**SALDI**	Sale
COMPLETO	Full	**SCONTO**	Discount
DA AFFITTARE	Fore hire	**SERVIZIO (NON) COMPRESO**	Service (not) included
DIVIETO	Prohibited	**SIGNORE**	Ladies
DIVIETO DI BAGNI	No bathing	**SIGNORI**	Gentlemen
DIVIETO DI TUFFARSI	No diving	**SI PUÒ FUMARE**	Smoking permitted
ENTRATA	Entrance	**SPESE**	Charges/Prices
ENTRATA LIBERA	Free entrance	**STANZE DA AFFITTARE**	Rooms to let
ESAURITO	Sold out	**STRADA PRIVATA**	Private road
FERMARE	Closed	**SUONARE PER FAVORE**	Please ring
FREDDO	Cold	**SVENDITA**	Sale
FUORI SERVIZIO	Out of order	**TOILETTE**	Toilets
GABINETTI	Toilets	**TRAGHETTO**	Ferry
GITE DI	Half-day tours	**USCITA**	Exit
-MEZZA GIORNATA		**USCITA EMERGENZA**	Emergency exit
GITE DI UN GIORNO	Full-day tours	**VENDUTO**	Sold out
GRATIS	Free	**VIETATO**	. . . Forbidden
GUASTO	Out of order	**VIETATO FUMARE**	No smoking
GUARDAROBA	Cloakroom	**VIETATO IL BAGNO/NUOTARE**	No bathing
INGRESSO GRATUITO	No obligation	**VIETATO SPORGERSI**	Don't lean out
I TRASGRESSORI	Trespassers will be	**VIETATO L'INGRESSO**	No entrance
-SARANNO PUNITI	prosecuted	**VIETATO TOCCARE**	Do not touch

for signs in stations & airports etc. see appropriate sections

In Length and Weight tables below, the middle figure can be read as metric or imperial measures; eg., 1 foot = 0.30 meters, or 1 meter = 3.3 feet.

LENGTH				**LENGTH**				**WEIGHT**	
feet		meters	inches		cms	lbs		kgs
3.3	1	0.30	0.4	1	2.5	2.2	1	0.45
6.6	2	0.61	0.8	2	5.0	4.4	2	0.90
9.9	3	0.91	1.2	3	7.6	6.6	3	1.4
13.1	4	1.22	1.6	4	10.6	8.8	4	1.8
16.4	5	1.52	2.0	5	12.7	11.0	5	2.2
19.7	6	1.83	2.4	6	15.2	13.2	6	2.7
23.0	7	2.13	2.8	7	17.8	15.4	7	3.2
26.2	8	2.44	3.2	8	20.3	17.6	8	3.6
29.5	9	2.74	3.5	9	22.9	19.8	9	4.1
32.9	10	3.05	4.0	10	25.4	22.0	10	4.5
			4.3	11	27.9			
			4.7	12	30.1			

DISTANCE/SPEED		**TEMPERATURE**		**FLUID MEASURE**			**TYRE PRESSURE**	
kms	miles	°C	°F	litrs	UK gal	US gal	lb/in²	kg/cm²
10	6	− 15	5	5	1.1	1.3	10	0.7
20	12	− 10	14	10	2.2	2.6	12	0.8
30	19	− 5	23	15	3.3	3.9	13	0.9
40	25	0	32	20	4.4	5.2	14	1.0
50	31	5	41	25	5.5	6.5	15	1.1
60	37	10	50	30	6.6	7.8	17	1.2
70	44	15	59	35	7.7	9.1	18	1.3
80	50	20	68	40	8.8	10.4	20	1.4
90	56	25	77	45	9.9	11.7	21	1.5
100	62	30	86	50	11.0	13.0	23	1.6
110	68	35	95	55	12.1	14.3	24	1.7
120	75	40	104	60	13.2	15.6	26	1.8
130	81	45	113	65	14.3	16.9	27	1.9
140	87	50	122	70	15.4	18.2	28	2.0
150	93	55	131	75	16.5	19.5	30	2.1
160	99	60	140	80	17.6	20.8	32	2.2
170	106	65	149	85	18.7	22.1	33	2.3
180	112	70	158	90	19.8	23.4	34	2.4
190	118	75	167	95	20.9	24.7	36	2.5
200	124	80	176	100	22.0	26.0	37	2.6
300	186	85	185				38	2.7
400	248	90	194				40	2.8
500	310	95	203					
1000	620	100	212					

for clothes sizes see: 38B

Here are the meanings of a few gestures you may come across in Italy which may not be familiar to you, or have different meanings to those you are used to. The precise meanings and degree of use can vary from area to area. Where alternatives are given, the first is the more common.

CHIN FLICK
= No *(Southern Italy)*
= Not Interested *(Nth)*

BACKHAND V-SIGN
= Victory
(not an insult!)

BACKWARD HEAD TOSS
= No
(Southern Italy only)

BACKHAND WIPE
= Go away!

FOREARM JERK
= Sexual Insult
(doesn't mean sexy!)

EYE PULL
= Watch Out!

BACKHAND WAVE
(Common way of waving hello or goodbye)

HAND-DOWN BECKON
= Come here

CHEEK SCREW
= Good!

FINGER PURSE
= Query

NOSE TAP
= Watch Out!
(Southern Italy only)

EAR PINCH
= Effeminate

?

I	*ee-yo* **IO**		
me	*may* **ME**		
he	*lwee* **LUI**		
she	*lay-ee* **LEI**		
we/us	*noy* **NOI**		
you	*lay-ee* **LEI**		
they/them	*lor-ro* **LORO**		
not	*non* **NON**		
no	*non* **NON**		

want	*vol-yo* **VOGLIO**	can I	*poss-o* **POSSO**
want	*vwar-lay* **VUOLE**	can I have	*poss-o ah-vair-ray* **POSSO AVERE**
have	*oh* **HO**	can we	*possee-yar-mo* **POSSIAMO**
have	*abbee-yar-mo* **ABBIAMO**	can we have	*possee-yar-mo ah-vair-ray* **POSSIAMO AVERE**
have	*ah* **HA**	can you	*pwoh* **PUÒ**
am	*so-no* **SONO**	Come	*ven-nee-ray* **VENIRE**
is	*eh* **È**	Go	*an-dar-ray* **ANDARE**
are	*so-no* **SONO**	Meet	*eencon-trar-ray* **INCONTRARE**
is it	*so-no* **SONO**	I'm Sorry	*mee deespee-yar-chay* **MI DISPIACE**
will be	*sar-rah* **SARÀ**	Wait	*aspet-tar-ray* **ASPETTARE**

which	*kwar-lay* **QUALE**
where	*doh-vay* **DOVE**
when	*kwan-doh* **QUANDO**
what	*koh-sa* **COSA**
what time	*kay or-ra* **CHE ORA**
how long	*kwan-toh tem-po* **QUANTO TEMPO**

Clock diagram:

minutes	pronunciation / Italian
0	*tsair-ro*
12	*doh-deechee*
1	*oo-no*
5 (at 1)	*cheen-kway*
2	*doo-way*
10	*dee-yay-chee*
3	*tray*
15	*kween-deechee*
4	*kwat-ro*
20	*ventee*
5	*cheen-kway*
25	*ventee cheen-kway*
6	*say-ee*
30	*tren-ta*
35	*trenta-cheen-kway*
7	*set-tay*
40	*kwar-ran-ta*
8	*ot-toh*
45	*kwarranta-cheen-kway*
9	*no-vay*
50	*cheen-kwan-ta*
10	*dee-yay-chee*
55	*cheenkwanta-cheen-kway*
11	*oon-deechee*

near	*vee-chee-no* **VICINO**
here	*kwee* **QUI**
there	*lar* **LÀ**
this	*kwess-toh* **QUESTO**

date	*dar-ta* **DATA**	appointment	*apoonta-men-toh* **APPUNTAMENTO**
birthday	*complay-yar-no* **COMPLEANNO**	meeting	*reeyoonee-yo-nay* **RIUNIONE**

ago *fah* **FA**	at *al* **AL**	from *dah* **DA**	in *een* **IN**	on *soo* **SU**	to *ah* **A**	too *trop-po* **TROPPO**

examples of saying time: at 5.30 = *allay* 5.30 at 7 o'clock = *allay* 7

first	*pree-mo* **PRIMO**	yesterday	*ee-yair-ree* **IERI**	Sunday	*dom-men-neeka* **DOMENICA**
next	*pross-seemo* **PROSSIMO**	today	*od-jee* **OGGI**	Monday	*loonay-dee* **LUNEDì**
last	*scor-so* **SCORSO**	tonight	*stan-not-tay* **STANOTTE**	Tuesday	*martay-dee* **MARTEDì**
early	*press-toh* **PRESTO**	tommorrow	*dom-mar-nee* **DOMANI**	Wednesday	*mairco-lay-dee* **MERCOLÉDì**
late	*een ree-tar-doh* **IN RITARDO**			Thursday	*jo-vay-dee* **GIOVEDì**
		morning	*mat-tee-no* **MATTINO**	Friday	*venair-dee* **VENERDì**
earlier	*pee-yoo press-toh* **PIÙ PRESTO**	midday	*metso-jor-no* **MEZZOGIORNO**	Saturday	*sar-battoh* **SABATO**
later	*pee-yoo tar-dee* **TARDI**	afternoon	*pommair-reed-jo* **POMERIGGIO**	weekday	*jor-no* *fairree-yar-lay* **GIORNO FERIALE**
now	*a-dess-so* **ADESSO**	evening	*sair-ra* **SERA**	weekend	*fee-nay* *settee-mar-na* **FINE SETTIMANA**
soon	*frah poc-ko* **FRA POCO**	night	*not-tay* **NOTTE**		
before	*pree-ma* **PRIMA**	midnight	*metsa-not-tay* **MEZZANOTTE**	January	*jen-I-yo* **GENNAIO**
after	*dor-po* **DOPO**			February	*febr-I-yo* **FEBBRAIO**
until	*fee-no ah* **FINO A**	seconds	*sec-kon-dee* **SECONDI**	March	*mart-so* **MARZO**
during	*doo-ran-tay* **DURANTE**	minutes	*mee-noo-tee* **MINUTI**	April	*ap-ree-lay* **APRILE**
since	*dah* **DA**	¼ of an hour	*kwar-toh dor-ra* **QUARTO D'ORA**	May	*mar-jo* **MAGGIO**
		½ an hour	*met-sor-ra* **MEZZ'ORA**	June	*joon-yo* **GIUGNO**
delay	*ree-tar-doh* **RITARDO**	hour	*or-ra* **ORA**	July	*lool-yo* **LUGLIO**
cancel	*canchel-lar-ray* **CANCELLARE**	day	*jor-no* **GIORNO**	August	*ag-goss-toh* **AGOSTO**
start	*ee-neet-seeyo* **INIZIO**	week	*setee-mar-na* **SETTIMANA**	September	*set-tem-bray* **SETTEMBRE**
finish	*fee-nay* **FINE**	month	*may-say* **MESE**	October	*ot-toh-bray* **OTTOBRE**
name	*no-may* **NOME**	years	*ar-nee* **ANNI**	November	*no-vem-bray* **NOVEMBRE**
address	*eendee-reet-so* **INDIRIZZO**	century	*sec-ko-lo* **SECOLO**	December	*dee-chem-bray* **DICEMBRE**

public holidays: 58A

0	**tsair**-ro	1000	**mee**-lay
1	**oo**-no	1100	meelay **chen**-toh
2	**doo**-way		
3	tray	2000	doo-way **mee**-la
4	**kwat**-ro	3000	tray **mee**-la
5	**cheen**-kway	4000	kwatro **mee**-la
6	**say**-ee	5000	cheenkway **mee**-la
7	**set**-tay		
8	**ot**-toh	100 000	chentoh **mee**-la
9	**no**-vay		
		1 000 000	oon meel-**yo**-nay

10	dee-**yay**-chee
11	**oon**-deechee
12	**doh**-deechee
13	**tray**-deechee
14	kwat-**tor**-deechee
15	**kween**-deechee
16	**say**-deechee
17	deecha-**set**-tay
18	dee-**chot**-oh
19	deecha-**no**-vay
20	**ven**-tee
21	vent **oo**-no
22	ventee **doo**-way
30	**tren**-ta
40	kwar-**ran**-ta
50	cheen-**kwan**-ta
60	sess-**san**-ta
70	set-**tan**-ta
80	ot-**tan**-ta
90	noh-**van**-ta
100	**chen**-toh
101	chentoh **oo**-no
110	chentoh dee-**yay**-chee
200	doo-way-**chen**-toh
300	tray-**chen**-toh
400	kwattro-**chen**-toh
500	cheenkway-**chen**-toh
600	say-**chen**-toh
700	settay-**chen**-toh
800	otto-**chen**-toh
900	no-vay-**chen**-toh

once	**oo**-na vol-**ta**	**UNA VOLTA**
twice	**doo**-way vol-**tay**	**DUE VOLTE**
five times	**cheen**-kway vol-**tay**	**CINQUE VOLTE**
a half	oon **met**-so	**UN MEZZO**
a quarter	oon **kwar**-toh	**UN QUARTO**
a third	oon **tairt**-so	**UN TERZO**
a pair	oon **pah**-eeyo	**UN PAIO**
a dozen	oona dotsee-na	**UNA DOZZINA**

A	ah	
B	bee	
C	chee	
D	dee	
E	ay	
F	**ef**-fay	
G	jee	
H	**ak**-ka	
I	ee	
J	ee-**loon**-go	
K	**kap**-pa	
L	**el**-ellay	
M	**em**-may	
N	**en**-nay	
O	oh	
P	pee	
Q	koo	
R	**air**-ray	
S	**ess**-ay	
T	tee	
U	oo	
V	voo	
W	**dop**-pee-oh-voo	
X	eex	
Y	ee-**grec**-ko	
Z	**tsay**-ta	

1st	**pree**-mo	1°
2nd	sec-**kon**-do	2°
3rd	**tairt**-so	3°
4th	**kwar**-toh	4°
5th	**kween**-toh	5°
6th	**sess**-toh	6°
7th	**set**-teemo	7°
8th	ot-**tar**-vo	8°
9th	**no**-no	9°
10th	**deh**-cheemo	10°
last	**ool**-teemo	**OOLTIMO**

1	1	1	1	1
2	2	2	2	2
3	3	3	3	3
4	4	4	4	4
5	5	5	5	5
6	6	6	6	6
7	7	7	7	7
8	8	8	8	8
9	9	9	9	9
0	0	0	0	0

PLEASE POINT OUT NUMBER
INDICARE NUMERO PER FAVORE